Children's Clothes

Children's Clothes

Since 1750

Clare Rose

B. T. BATSFORD LIMITED, LONDON

Dedication
For my Grandmothers

First published 1989
© Clare Rose 1989

ISBN 0 7134 5741 4

Typeset by Keyspools Ltd.,
Golborne, Lancs
Printed in Great Britain by
Courier International, Tiptree, Essex

for the publishers
B. T. Batsford Limited,
4 Fitzhardinge Street,
London W1H 0AH

Contents

Acknowledgements

I would like to thank all of the friends and colleagues who helped me with the research and writing of this book, many of whom have been extremely generous with their time and information. Foremost among them are: Penelope Byrde and Myra Mines of the Museum of Costume, Bath; Kate Brown and Sarah Rayner of Bristol Museums; Noreen Marshall of the Bethnal Green Museum of Childhood; Liz Arthur of the Museum of Costume, Glasgow; Kay Staniland, Cathie Collcutt and Jill Spanner of the Museum of London; Anthea Jarvis, Miles Lambert and Philip Sykas of the Gallery of English Costume, Manchester; Naomi Tarrant of the National Museum of Scotland; Elizabeth Earle of The National Trust, Killerton House; Jeremy Farrell and Suella Postles of Nottingham Museums; Jane Arthur and Liz Salmon of the City Museum and Art Gallery, Stoke-on-Trent; and the Director and staff of York Castle Museum.

For permission to reproduce paintings, drawings and photographs in their collections I should like to thank Her Majesty the Queen; Mr John Chichester-Constable; Mothercare PLC; Grattan PLC; Hamlyn Ltd; Chatto and Windus Ltd; The National Museum of Film, Photography and Television; The Tate Gallery; The Witt Library, The Courtauld Institute of Art; the Syndics of the Fitzwilliam Museum, Cambridge; Leeds City Art Galleries; The Detroit Institute of Arts; The Minneapolis Institute of Arts; The Yale Center for British Art (Paul Mellon Collection).

For their help in researching eighteenth- and nineteenth-century paintings, I would like to thank Evelyn Newby of the Mellon Research Centre and David Alexander. Eric Smith, Joanna Hashagen and Johnathan Newdick helped to develop the child-sized figures which appear in some of the photographs, while Lucinda Douglas-Menzies and Richard Stansfield assisted with the photography itself. The cost of my travel in undertaking this research was funded by a generous grant from the Pasold Foundation.

For guiding this book from inception to publication, I would like to thank Dr Aileen Ribeiro and the editorial staff at Batsford.

Finally, I would like to thank my family, and especially my husband, for their help and support throughout this project.

List of Plates

(between pages 96 and 97)

List of Illustrations

Introduction

The history of children's clothes has sometimes been dismissed as a matter of 'babygowns and old lace', of interest only to the specialist. This could hardly be further from the truth. Like the other major branches of costume history, the study of children's clothes acts as a window through which we can gain insights into the history of culture and ideas, and into economic history. An understanding of the clothes worn in a particular period is vital to the interpretation of the paintings, literature and accounts of that date. In addition to these insights, children's clothes shed light on areas not covered by adult fashion. These include theories of child-care, the philosophy of education, and the position of children in society. Children's clothing also escapes some of the adult standards of fashion and of propriety, and can act as a testing ground of new styles and methods of construction.

In selecting material for this book I have stayed within the mainstream of children's fashion. I have tried to show the relationships of children's clothes both to adult fashions and to social and economic trends. Some aspects of the clothing industry, such as the babywear produced around Glasgow in the early nineteenth century, can be taken as a microcosm of Britain's industrial history. The book contains information of interest to historians of portraiture, economic historians and social historians, as well as those studying costume for its own sake. Much of the surviving evidence is inevitably slanted towards upper-class children, but I have balanced this by including extracts from working-class autobiographies.

The book begins in 1750, which represents a watershed between old and new ways of looking at children. The old view was of children as imperfect copies of adults, needing physical restraint to direct their development. In the new view, children were individuals, possessing qualities – such as innocence – not normally found in adults. This view, which stressed the needs of young children for special types of food, clothing and education, gradually triumphed and has informed attitudes to children until the present. Legal and social distinctions between adults and children have only been made since the nineteenth century; in earlier periods, quite young children lived in ways which we would consider adult. This is especially true of poorer children, who might be expected to put in a working day of 14 hours from the age of 5. The age at which 'childhood' ended varied according to the circumstances of the families, as well as over time.

One of the interesting aspects of children's clothing is the light it casts on contemporary ideas of childhood. These ideas may be supported or disproved when we look at the evidence of surviving garments. The sizes of the garments themselves, and their tightness of fit, can offer some guidance to the degree of activity allowed to their wearers. The materials, construction and methods of manufacture often anticipate or reinforce new trends in adult clothing. This is especially true of mass-produced garments, whose origins can be traced to the Ayrshire work babygowns of the early nineteenth century.

Children's clothes have always been allowed an element of fantasy which is usually absent from adult dress. The form this fantasy takes is carefully chosen; young boys have often been dressed in clothing derived from army or navy uniforms. Girls' clothes have tended to exaggerate some aspect of adult fashion and are often shorter, brighter and frillier than their mothers'. The significance of clothes is often modified by the way they are depicted in paintings or photographs; when apparently simple clothes appear in lavish settings we must revise our ideas about their simplicity!

Instruction books for needlework or babycare provide invaluable guides to interpreting surviving garments. They tell us not only what the garment was called, what it was made of and how, but also what age and social class of child would wear it. Some of the early books have separate instructions for 'ladies' children' and 'children of the poor'. Later guides are less socially divisive, but still contain insights into the context in which garments would be worn. The hard work required by laundry day and the advisability of holding it as infrequently as possible is emphasised by nineteenth century books' recommendations for layettes of 'a dozen of everything'.

The importance of clothing in children's upbringing is stressed again and again by autobiographers in the nineteenth and early twentieth century. Strictly brought up girls remember the corsets and tight shoes intended to turn them into 'young ladies'. Girls starting work were often expected to provide suitable clothing, and this could determine what jobs they were able to take. Well into the twentieth century, the cost of special clothing acted as a deterrent to children offered 'free' places at grammar schools. Even among children from similar backgrounds, unsuitable or inadequate clothing often was (and is) an excuse for teasing and social ostracism.

The changing cost and variety of children's clothes is particularly evident in the flysheets and catalogues produced for large retailers and mail-order firms throughout the twentieth century. The growth of mail-order from the 1920s onwards did a great deal to level prices and distribute fashions throughout Britain. The catalogues contain subtle indications of the social standing of their clients; this can be seen very clearly in the variety and cost of baby clothes on offer. From the evidence of these catalogues, it seems as if children's clothes have gradually become cheaper in real terms. There is certainly more choice available now at the lower end of the price-range than there was a century ago. Recently the levelling trend has been reversed, and we are now seeing 'designer' garments for infants.

In preparing this book I looked at a great variety of surviving garments and of written and painted records in order to choose those which gave the clearest picture of the development of children's clothing. Material can be found in photograph albums, in paintings, in novels, in letters and diaries, in schoolbooks, in museum collections and in bottom drawers. I have often used several sources together in order to bring out the information contained in an object. For example, an old school photograph can be explained using the reminiscences of someone who attended a similar school, and given further interest by a page from a mail-order catalogue showing the cost of the garments worn. A pile of anonymous white baby garments can be interpreted using a 'mothercraft' book of the same date, or notes prepared for Domestic Science lessons. Clothing is a very direct way back to the past and to other peoples' lives, and can prompt both the reminiscences of older people and the interest of children. I hope that this book will both inform and provide a framework for further enquiry.

CHAPTER ONE

Babies: 1750-1820

Infants are tender twigs and as you use them, so they will grow straight or crooked.
Jane Sharp, *The Midwives' Book*, 1671

In 1750, the traditional attitude to babies and young children could be summed up in the saying 'As the twig is bent, so grows the tree'. Taken literally, this was one of the main rationales behind the practice of swaddling, practised in Europe since Roman times, and surviving in some areas until the 1920s. It was thought that young babies might catch cold or injure themselves if allowed unrestrained exercise. They were therefore dressed in a way that allowed no more movement than a turn of the head – sometimes not even that (Fig. 1).

The first garments put on for swaddling were a fine linen shirt, open down the front or back, and a long 'bellyband' of strong fabric which was wrapped round the body to suppress the navel and support the abdomen (Fig. 2). The nappy or 'napkin' would be a square of linen cloth, possibly in fine 'diaper' weave. Both adults' and children's undergarments were made of linen until well into the nineteenth century, as it is a fibre which absorbs body moisture well and can be boiled in washing. On its head the infant would have one or even two linen caps, with perhaps a triangular forehead piece for added warmth and decoration. The neck and shoulders of the shirt and the edges and crown of the cap might be trimmed with lace, which might have been either imported Valenciennes or homemade hollie point.

Over these standard items went the swaddling clothes themselves. The first was a large rectangle known as a 'bed' which was wrapped round the child's body, holding its arms straight against its sides, turned up over the feet and pinned in place (Fig. 3). At this date straight pins were the only fastening available for infants' clothes apart from stitching or drawstrings. Formerly swaddling bands, strips of linen about two inches (5 cm) wide had been wound round the child to keep the 'bed' in place; but these are not shown in depictions of eighteenth-century infants. If they were used, then another 'bed' would be pinned over the top to make a sausage-shaped parcel. The final piece was the 'stayband', a strip of linen placed under the cap and pinned to the clothes at shoulder level to keep the head straight. Extras might be added in the form

George Romney, Mrs Johnstone and Child, 1775–80. The young child wears one of the simple linen dresses trimmed with tucks which were favoured in the late eighteenth century. The ties fastening the open back can be clearly seen.

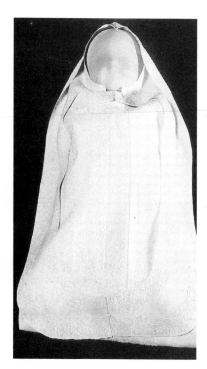

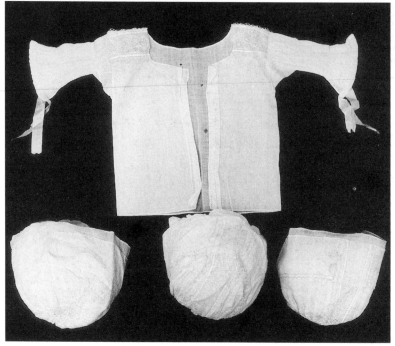

Fig. 1   A fully swaddled baby of the
late seventeenth or early eighteenth
century. The set of swaddling clothes
consists of a 'bed', 'long stay' and
collar (two pieces not shown). All are
made of linen, with a pattern in
applied cord.

Fig. 2   A shirt and three caps worn by
the infant Lord North in 1732. All are
trimmed with insertions of hollie point
and have impressed patterns executed
by the laundress.

Fig. 3   A diagram showing the
different stages involved in swaddling a
newborn baby. The nappy was
probably made into a triangle, but
could also be folded in a rectangle and
wrapped around the body and each
leg. Older babies would have their
arms left free.

Fig. 4 Part of a mid eighteenth-century swaddling set. The 'long stay' and sleeves are made of linen, decorated with folded strips of fabric. Length 21 inches (53 cm).

of bibs and collars which tied round the neck. Sometimes the 'stayband' was extended downwards to frame the front of the baby's body, in which case it was called a 'long stay'.

These outer pieces were decorated using washable techniques; a favourite trimming in the late seventeenth and early eighteenth centuries was scrolling patterns of applied cord (Fig. 1). It is difficult to describe mid eighteenth-century sets as very few survive (Fig. 4). It may be that when swaddling was finally given up it was only the earlier, 'heirloom' sets of swaddling clothes that were kept, along with the reusable pieces such as shirts and caps.

Attacks on swaddling had already begun by 1750; one of the first was contained in the book *An Essay on Nursing*, published in 1748. The author, Dr William Cadogan, was a London doctor known for his work in orphanages. He objected to the practice because 'limbs, that are not used, will never be strong, and such tender bodies cannot bear much pressure.'[1] This was followed by an even more influential diatribe in J. J. Rousseau's *Emile*, first published in 1762. Rousseau took many of his theories from John Locke's *Some Thoughts Concerning Education*, 1693, which had put forward the idea that babies and children were healthier when they were 'hardened' to the elements by lightweight clothing and cold baths. Rousseau added a political element to the criticism of children's clothing, and saw in swaddling clothes the first of the many institutions which bind men to virtual 'slavery': 'The infant is bound up in swaddling clothes, the corpse is nailed down in his coffin'.[2] Advice against swaddling is continued in childcare books of the late eighteenth century and early nineteenth century, though often with such disclaimers as 'the very ancient tight mode of dressing...[now] discontinued'.[3]

With so many objectors, it may seem odd that swaddling had survived so long. It did so because it fitted not only parents' theories, but also their practical needs. Eighteenth-century childbirth was a hazardous process for both mother and child, whose 'bones, or joints, may be sometimes unavoidably injured in the birth'.[4] The suggested remedy was cardboard splints and tight clothing, but swaddling could also give the desired effect. Even after birth, there were some cases in which the child's chances of survival could be improved by the restraints of swaddling. Many agricultural and industrial processes were still carried out in the home, where cramped living conditions, large items of machinery and open fires created a potentially dangerous environment. One reason why swaddling was continued longer in poor families was that it gave the parents 'time to attend to other concerns, who are obliged to work for their bread'.[5] Swaddling would also be appreciated for the calming effect it had on babies.[6] Nineteenth-century working mothers still needed to keep their children quiet while they earned their living; but the nineteenth-century choice of sedative was laudanum, a mixture of opium and alcohol. This was far more harmful to the children than any form of physical restraint.

Even when swaddling was practised as a matter of course, its duration may not have been long enough to hurt the child; its arms were generally freed after a few weeks, and the whole process might be left off after two to four months.[7]

Once it was out of swaddling, a baby in arms would wear a long dress with sleeves turned back at the elbow, with a shirt and petticoats underneath. Unfortunately babies of the 1750s were often painted wearing bibs which hide the front of their dresses. If they could be seen, they would probably look like Fig. 5. This is one of a pair of baby dresses, printed in indigo on linen, which are among the earliest to survive. The printed pattern meant that they would show the dirt less, and need less frequent washing. This was no small consideration in a period when soap was taxed as a 'luxury' item.[8]

The first examples of special Christening gowns also date from the 1750s and 1760s. Previously, a 'bearing cloth' had been wrapped round the swaddled child for the duration of the ceremony. This was a large piece of heavy silk up to nine feet (2.7 m) square, trimmed round the edges with gold lace and braid. With babies coming out of swaddling at a younger age, a different type of dress was needed for the ceremony (Fig. 6). These were made from a single piece of silk satin, left open down the front, and tucked for about five inches (13 cm) to form a semi-fitted bodice. The shoulder straps were made of separate pieces, giving a low front and back neck, while the set-in sleeves were usually short with a turned-back cuff. The fronts and hem were often decorated with wavy lines of silk braid and fringing similar to those seen on women's dresses in the 1760s and 1770s. The fronts were sometimes closed with ribbon ties, or might be pinned with non-functional ribbon bows. Sometimes the fronts were left open to show a matching petticoat.

Other special garments for older babies were simply cut robes of silk quilted over lambswool wadding. These were cut in a flared shape, opening down the front, and with detachable sleeves (Fig. 7). Their warmth would be much appreciated in chilly country houses, especially when paired with quilted cradle covers and hangings.[9] Quilting was also used for smaller items such as caps and jackets. For these the favoured technique was corded quilting worked on linen (Fig. 8), which gave strength and patterning rather than warmth. Small pieces such as these might be made from the good portions of an adult's waistcoat or a worn-out bedcover, though this would make the seams rather bulky.

Up to the 1740s the toddler just out of baby clothes wore a dress similar to those of its mother, of silk for those who could afford it, homespun wool or linen for others. These had a tightly fitted bodice which was boned or worn over stiff stays, with a low neck and elbow-length sleeves. The full skirt was made separately and gathered onto a tape at the waist (Fig. 9). The only sign of childhood was that the bodice fastened at the back, unlike a woman's, making it even more difficult for the child to dress itself! These

Fig. 5   A 'slip' babydress, probably mid eighteenth-century. Bodice and skirt are made of two pieces of coarse block-printed linen, pleated into shape. The bodice is lined. Length 31 inches (79 cm).

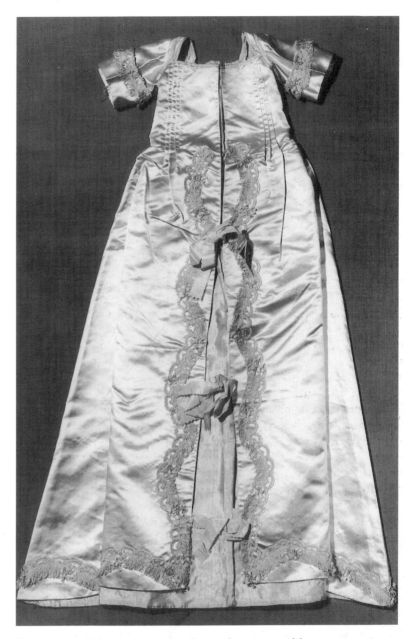

Fig. 6   A lavish 'slip' gown of cream silk satin, made for a christening in 1760 to 1780. Open down the front, it is trimmed with silk braid and ribbons, and lined with fine silk. Length 34 inches (86 cm).

dresses would be worn with a linen chemise cut like a woman's, an under-petticoat, stockings and shoes. Toddlers just learning to walk would wear a protective head-dress called a 'pudding' (Fig. 11). This was a roll of padded cloth which resembled a black pudding. It was tied round the head with ribbons.

A further reminder of childish status could be seen in the 'leading strings', long strips of material attached to the shoulders of the dress. These originally derived from the decorative hanging sleeves worn on sixteenth-century robes, but were retained for both their practical and their symbolic function. Girls were often said to be 'in leading strings', that is under parental guidance, up

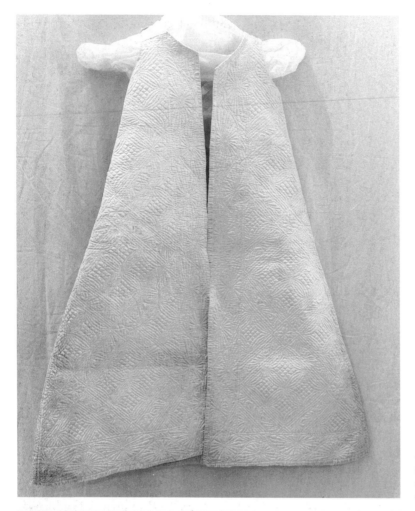

Fig. 7 *A quilted silk robe made for a christening in the 1760s, and worn afterwards for warmth. It would have had sleeves pinned or sewn on.*

Fig. 8 *Three linen caps worked in corded quilting in both 'all-over' and 'motif' techniques. The simple three-piece construction was often used with bulky fabrics. Mid eighteenth-century.*

Fig. 9   A toddler's dress of the 1740s, using silk woven in Spitalfields, London. The bodice and skirt are separate, and the bodice is lined. No leading strings. Length 26.5 inches (67 cm).

to their teens, and might be portrayed wearing them. But not all surviving dresses have leading strings (even those which would fit 2-year-olds), so the portraits may have been symbolic not realistic. Up to the age of 4 or 5, boys were dressed 'in petticoats' like their sisters (Fig. 10). A distinction between the sexes would be maintained by degrees of trimming and jewellery, in the fit of the bodice (tighter for a girl, looser for a boy), and, most importantly, by headgear. Boys might wear a large feathered hat or go bareheaded, while girls were more likely to be restricted to a close fitting cap. Sometimes these were made completely of ruched lace and ribbon (Fig. 28).

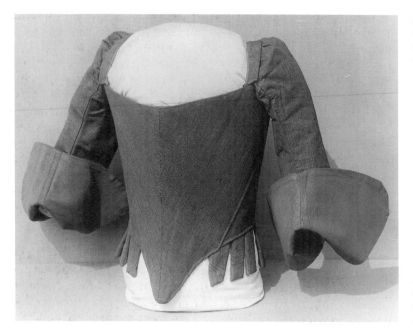

Fig. 10   *A bodice of dark red wool with silk facings, made for a boy born in 1725. It is fully boned, with a waist of 17 inches (43 cm).*

Fig. 11 (below)   *A 'pudding' cap made of red velvet, padded and quilted, with red silk lining and ties. Circumference 41.5 inches (62 cm).*

The Age of Sensibility

In the last two decades of the eighteenth century there was a change in manners and ideals which ushered in the 'Age of Sensibility'.[10] This was due partly to the persistence of the 'back to nature' ideal advocated by reformers such as Rousseau, and partly to the heady notions of liberty and 'natural rights' planted by the founders of the new French and American republics. Although these ideas might be dangerous if carried to excess, they did have some effect on popular opinion. English society of the late eighteenth century was considered remarkably egalitarian by many foreign commentators.[11] Middle-class, not courtly values dominated English society, given the lead by King George III and Queen Charlotte, who raised 15 children in quiet domesticity.

This increasing respect for individual liberties and for domestic values had an influence both on the treatment and on the dress of children. While attitudes to infants may not have changed, they were expressed much more freely and affectionately. From the 1760s onwards, we find baby clothes and accessories with sentimental inscriptions such as 'long live sweet babe' (1765), 'long live the babe' (1769) and 'sweet bab don't cry'.[12] These inscriptions were usually executed in small panels of hollie point lace (whose looped technique made it suited to counted patterns) for insertion in baby shirts or caps. They were also executed in pins on decorative silk pincushions for the layette basket. By contrast, earlier eighteenth century pincushions and caps gave just initials and a date, sometimes accompanied by important dynastic information such as the names and status of the parents.

The importance of children and babies to the domestic ideal is borne out by the frequency with which they appear in late eighteenth-century paintings, both formal portraits and genre scenes. Benjamin West's portrait of his own family, from which a detail is shown in Fig. 12, illustrates the ideal of intimacy between mother and children. Formerly there had been some doubt as to the spiritual status of children; were they 'limbs of Satan' or messengers from a purer world? By 1800 the latter view had won over, helped by the advocacy of the Romantic poets, particularly Blake.

As if to emphasize their innocence, babies and young children were increasingly dressed completely in white with ribbon sashes as the only colour. This choice owed much to the newly fashionable nature of linen and cotton fabrics. Plain linen for sheets and underwear had been produced in Britain for centuries, but from 1750 onwards improvements in printing techniques made it a fashionable fabric for rich and poor alike.[13] The success of the linen industry laid the foundation for the cotton mills set up in the 1780s in Lancashire and the west of Scotland. New technology for spinning and weaving the cotton fibres produced fabrics which rivalled the fine muslins imported from Bengal.[14]

By the late 1780s, a popular dress for women was the 'chemise gown' of plain white muslin, loosely cut and gathered with drawstrings. Although these white dresses may have appeared simple and egalitarian in comparison to the silk brocades of an earlier period, they were still relatively expensive to make, fragile in wear, and troublesome in upkeep. Consequently the 1780s, which saw the ascendancy of the white cotton muslin dress for well-to-do children, also saw the establishment at a poorer level of society of the printed cotton or linen dress, made of a fabric that was both stronger and less vulnerable to soiling. One painting which shows this difference is Fig. 21. The printed or coloured cotton dress, worn under a simple overall made from a large piece of cloth with two armholes, was to remain one of the distinguishing marks of the 'cottage' child until the late nineteenth century (Fig. 58).

The white dresses worn by children took two main forms. One was the 'bib-fronted' dress, with a tight-fitting bodice with a

Fig. 12 (left) The Artist's Family *(detail), Benjamin West, c. 1772. The baby wears a 'slip' dress and close fitting cap, the mother a loose wrapping gown, and the older boy an 'English' suit (see Chapter 3).*

Fig. 13 (right) A 'slip' gown of strong *cotton trimmed with tamboured muslin, c. 1770–90. The 'petticoat' effect is given by a front panel. Length 40.5 inches (103 cm).*

pointed waist. A triangular panel was outlined by tucks or cord on the bodice front, imitating the stomachers of women's dresses. This style had been in use since the 1740s as an alternative to stiffer wool and silk. It could be made of semi-sheer linen cambric, and was sometimes worn over a contrasting coloured petticoat. It was usually made in one piece, with an open back seam.[15]

The other style of white dress worn by toddlers was simply a larger version of the 'slip' dresses worn by babies. These had become standard wear with the demise of swaddling, and were being made in fine cambric and muslin as well as heavy linen (Fig. 13). Because of their simple tucked construction it was easy

Fig. 14   A 'slip' of cotton twill, trimmed with fringing, c. 1770–90. It opens both at the back and on either side of the buttoned front panel. There may originally have been a cord laced between the buttons. Length 32 inches (81 cm).

to scale them up for larger children, or even to let them out as the child grew. When made for older children they were given a little more trimming; a favourite method was to place two rows of buttons on the bodice and join them with a 'laced' cord. This gave the effect of the frogging seen on hussars' uniforms, which were a favourite source for eighteenth-century fancy dress (Fig. 14). Muslin dresses might be given several tucks at the hem which were both decorative and functional. Little boys' slips might have a slit from waist to hem at the front, giving them more freedom of movement.[16]

As the eighteenth century drew to a close, the desire of adults to seek inspiration from 'nobler' eras of the past led to an adoption of 'classical' styles of dress. Both women's and men's clothes assumed a closeness to the body, and a revealing quality which had been absent from fashionable dress for centuries. Dresses were made of softly draping fabrics such as muslin, were high waisted and seemingly uncorseted, and evening dresses left both neck and arms exposed.

The supposed parallels between women's drapery and classical styles were deliberately emphasized by the Revolutionary govern-

Fig. 15   A baby's pelisse of striped cotton trimmed with muslin frills, c. 1780–1800. It is double-breasted for greater warmth. Similar styles were worn by girls and women (see Fig. 24). Length 39 inches (100 cm).

ment of France, eager to create a new state modelled on Ancient Rome. Yet the Empire and Regency styles of 1790–1820 can also be seen as a transference to women's dress of some of the qualities of late eighteenth-century children's clothes. These were lightness in weight and brevity of cut, with chest and arms exposed, and pale colours. The idea of 'hardening', which favoured scanty clothes for children, found its counterpart in an admiration for classical stoicism.

These new styles, however soundly based in archaeology, were even less suited to the British climate than was the Roman toga. Innumerable compromises were adopted in the shape of multiple petticoats, long sleeves to tie on shoulder capes, and even full-length coats for outings (Fig. 15). Hampered by the drawstrings of dress and petticoat, of mittens, tippet and cap, and by their narrow skirts, it is a wonder that well-dressed children had the energy for the boisterous play shown in contemporary prints.

Like all movements based on ideals, the taste for neo-classical simplicity had to come to an end. From the outset, muslin manufacturers had used small sprigged patterns, either woven or embroidered, to add interest and value to their wares.[17] By 1800, dressmakers were using insertions of fine lace or darned net to edge and define the shapes of dresses and caps. Early muslins were loosely-woven, and were suited to decoration with pulled stitches akin to the Dresdenwork popular in the mid eighteenth century. This type of work could be extremely decorative when combined with shadow embroidery and satin stitch (Fig. 16).

By 1820, the picture presented by the fashionable baby was not one of classical simplicity but came close to the Romantic frilliness of contemporary female dress. Some plainer styles did survive, such as 'hussar' dresses, their bodices trimmed with rows of braid and buttons in imitation of women's outdoor dress (Fig. 38). There had been losses as well as gains in the years since 1750. Swaddling had finally been abandoned, and the infant's need for a greater degree of freedom and of cleanliness had been recognized. Older children's clothing was lighter and less constricting than it had been in mid-century; but the flimsy muslin dresses must have constituted a direct trial of the theory of hardening. The effect of freedom was also somewhat spoiled by the multitude of extra garments needed to come to terms with British weather.

Finally, by 1820 a new garment had been added to the wardrobe of both women and children; drawers. These took several forms: sometimes they were attached to a tape at the waist, sometimes to a bodice with shoulder straps. Sometimes they were only 'leglets', with no other function than to cover the ankle. Adult women had turned to drawers to provide decency without bulk under narrow-cut dresses; children had even more need of them, as for the first time their dresses were being worn substantially shorter than their elders' (see front jacket illustration).

CHAPTER TWO

Girls: 1750-1820

The Bennett Family, *Samuel Woodforde, 1803. This painting shows the similarities between women's and children's dress in the early nineteenth century. The classical effect of the dresses is heightened by their light colours and restrained decoration. The younger boy wears a skeleton suit; the older one has a miniature tailcoat.*

In 1750, there were apparently two ways of dealing with young girls' clothing. The first was to keep them in the back-fastening, bib-fronted dresses of childhood until their early teens. They would then proceed directly to a front-opening silk dress of the same quality, and with the same accessories, as their mother.

The difference a few years could make is shown clearly in the portrait of Sir Edward Walpole's children, painted in 1747 by Stephen Slaughter (Fig. 18). The two younger girls, aged 9 and 11, are shown wearing plain light-coloured dresses, probably of linen, with loose elbow-length sleeves and a bodice with a front panel outlined by tucks or applied cord. This is the dress seen in portraits of young children from 1740 onwards.[1] Like them, it is back fastening and made in two pieces, so that the apron is worn tucked under the point of the bodice. The bodices are much more closely fitted than a toddler's would be, however, and are worn over tight stays to give the required tapering waist.

The clothes worn by their elder sister Laura, aged 13, present a complete contrast. Her dress is made of an expensive brocaded silk, not linen, and is made in one piece. It is front-opening, with pleated 'robings' framing a contrasting stomacher trimmed with bows. Her muslin apron, shaped to fit her pointed waistline, ties over her bodice, not under it. And as a final sign of her status, the neck and cuffs of her chemise are edged with lace, while her sisters make do with muslin or lawn.

The alternative way of dressing girls was to provide a series of stages between babyhood and adulthood. This could be done by giving them dresses which resembled women's in their proportions, fabric and trimming, but were distinguished by childish details. Two of the most important signs of childhood were the back-opening bodice and leading strings. Back-opening, stiffened bodices had been worn by women in the seventeenth and early eighteenth centuries, but by the 1740s were only used for extremely formal Court dress. Why they were thought suitable for children is a mystery; perhaps they gave a neater appearance.

Leading strings are even more mysterious. When they appear on

Irene Home

Fig. 17 (*left*)   Anne Hoare, *William Hoare, c. 1750.* In this drawing the artist's young daughter is wearing a patterned silk or linen gown with a back fastening and leading-strings. A sheer apron covers the front of the dress. The scarf wrapped round the neck and over the decorated cap is an unusual detail.

Fig. 18 (*below*)   The Children of Sir Edward Walpole, *Stephen Slaughter, 1747.* The sitters are Laura (age 13), Maria (age 11), Charlotte (age 9) and Edward (age 10). There is a great contrast between the plain cotton or linen dresses of the younger girls and their elder sister's silk brocade. All three wear small caps trimmed with ribbon and lace, but only Laura has lace edging her chemise. Edward's suit is of velvet and satin (see Chapter 3).

toddlers' dresses, they are clearly functional. When used for older girls approaching adulthood, they symbolize dependence on parental guidance. They appear to have been worn with formal silk dresses only, not the linen dresses of everyday wear.[2] They were not universally worn; some surviving dresses such as Fig. 9 do not have them, nor are they shown on all portraits.

Where leading-strings are present, the dress is often richly trimmed, like Fig. 19. This dress of patterned blue silk is made in one piece, with the skirt pleated into the pointed waist. The skirt is

Fig. 19   A small girl's dress of blue silk woven with a zig-zag pattern, c. 1760–80. The bodice is lined with linen and boned at the back opening. Bodice, skirt and leading strings are trimmed with silver lace. This was obviously intended for a young child, as there is a matching pudding cap. Front length 35 inches (58 cm).

Fig. 20 A girl's dress of yellow and pink satin, c. 1770–80. The fabric has been used to emphasize the cut of the bodice. The skirt is quilted over wool wadding. There is a second matching bodice, sleeveless and with a frill at bust and waist. Length 35 inches (89 cm).

six inches longer at the back; some of this length would be held out by petticoats with the remainder forming a train. The bodice is lined with linen but not stiffened, apart from two strips of whalebone on either side of the back opening. The dress is decorated on the bodice and sleeves and down the flat front of the skirt with scrolls of silver lace. The scrolls themselves, and the way in which they are placed, echo the decoration of women's dresses in the 1770s (see Fig. 28). At the same time, the construction of the dress, the presence of leading strings and of a 'pudding' trimmed to match, remind us that this is a small girl's garment.

Not all silk dresses were as lavish as Fig. 19, however. Those which appear in portraits of the 1760s and 1770s are more often made without any trimming. A decorative element was supplied by embroidered muslin cuffs and apron (see Fig. 28). The apron was a favourite informal accessory for English women; Queen Charlotte herself wore one, to the surprise of foreign visitors.[3] Women's aprons, however, always ended at the waist, like Laura Walpole's in Fig. 18. The bib of girls' aprons supplied a decorative focus to the front of the dress, in place of the stomacher of women's dresses. Bibbed aprons shared the symbolic role of leading strings: 'Ev'n misses at whose age their mothers wore/The backstring and the bib' – Cowper, *The Task*, 1785.[4]

A surviving example of one of these plainer silk dresses is seen in Fig. 20. It is made of satin striped in pink and yellow with the fabric used diagonally on the bodice front, and sideways on the sleeves. The skirt is quilted over wool wadding to give both warmth and fashionable fullness.

The rarity of surviving children's garments from this period is extremely unfortunate, as it makes us even more dependent on the contradictory evidence of portraits. These have an inbuilt bias, both from the nature of the sitters (wealthy), and from the way they chose to be recorded (at their best). Different families wished to present themselves with different degrees of formality, as can be seen by contrasting portraits from the same artist.[5]

Artists also had their preferences: Devis preferred to paint satins in a period when flowered silks were the height of fashion. The puffed cap with a hanging 'tail' worn by the girl in Fig. 28 may be an invention of Wheatley's; it appears in several of his portraits, but not elsewhere.[6] Perhaps the safe conclusion to be drawn from the clothes shown in eighteenth-century portraits is that they represent styles which both subject and artist found acceptable, and were not necessarily from the sitter's actual wardrobe.

The very informal outdoor portraits which became popular in the 1770s, showing families fishing or boating, are misleading in another way.[7] The apparently simple white dresses worn with such insouciant ease by girls on river banks were in fact deceptively expensive both to make and to maintain.

Cotton, though less expensive than silk, was imported from India until the 1780s and was priced accordingly. Linen was manufactured in Britain, but cloth of the fineness shown in these paintings required great expertise in both spinning and weaving. Soft cotton muslin was even less durable than fine linen lawn, and much less so than the stiff dress silks of the period. Washing, though carried out infrequently, would further shorten the life of a muslin dress. They were generally unsuitable for remodelling, once their first use was over; early nineteenth-century examples often have carefully worked darns. All of these factors help to explain why the simple white dress is often paired with incongruously rich silk sashes or with elaborate caps made up of puffs of lace, ribbon and gauze.[8] Sometimes, too, the sheer white fabric is set off by a coloured silk underdress, as in Colour Plate 1. The muslin aprons of Fig. 18 and Fig. 28 are also enhanced by the dark silk of the dresses beneath. The combination of sheer overdress and coloured underdress returned to popularity for formal wear in the early nineteenth century.

It is not surprising, then, that late eighteenth-century prints and paintings showing poorer children do not include many white dresses. Girls, whether living on farms or in the rapidly-growing cities, appear to have worn a simple one-piece dress of coloured linen or linen mixture. This is often shown tucked or pinned up to the waist to protect its 'right' side, revealing a darker-coloured petticoat probably made of wool.

Older girls are seen wearing a stiffened leather bodice over a linen chemise, and coloured petticoats. This form of corset worn as an outer garment had been traditional throughout the peasant societies of Europe since at least the sixteenth century. By the 1780s this custom was on the wane in England, both for adults and children, and it had practically died out by the early nineteenth century.[9] Where the leather bodice and petticoat is shown in paint-

Fig. 21   Blind Man's Buff, George Morland, 1787. This painting was part of a series showing children's games, intended for publication as prints. There is a contrast between the wealthy children in the centre, and the poorer children in the background. Points of interest are the simple pinafores worn by the children on the left, and the large scarf worn as an apron by 'it' (see Fig. 26).

ings of the 1780s, it may be attributed to the artist's idea of what country girls should wear, rather than to direct observation.

By the 1790s, a more typical outfit for cottage girls was the one-piece dress of printed cotton or linen, worn under a pinafore of plain fabric. This combination is seen in George Morland's painting *Blind Man's Buff* (Fig. 21), commissioned by a print dealer as part of a series showing children's games.[10] The print dresses and pinafores of the cottage children are contrasted with the white dresses and silk sashes of their wealthier companions. The pinafores are simply made from a single piece of fabric with slits for armholes and a drawstring at the neck. This pattern was still a favourite in the late nineteenth century. While they were effective in hiding the clothes beneath them from dirt, they are frustrating to the costume historian for the same reason. One has to assume that poorer children's dress followed the general lines of fashion.

The 'chemise dress' and neo-classicism

By the 1780s, fashionable women's dress was showing radical changes. The first of these was the increasing acceptance of plain or printed cotton and linen fabrics for informal wear. This may have been prepared for by the popularity of linen dresses for children, but the second development is less easily explained. This was the new 'chemise dress' made of fine white linen or cotton like the undergarment of the same name. It was cut very fully, with the fullness controlled by drawstrings at the neck, bust and waist. It was at first thought shocking for its transparency, its flimsy construction and its resemblance to underwear. However it gradually gained acceptance after it was taken up by Queen Marie Antoinette and the ladies of the French Court.[11]

Paintings of this dress on adults are rare, and only a single example survives in England.[12] It seems to have found much wider acceptance for young girls. By 1790 it is the most commonly depicted style, and the bib-fronted dresses of the mid eighteenth century are nowhere to be seen. The outline of the dress might be varied by short or long sleeves, which could be left plain or gathered in puffs like the bodice (Fig. 22). Common trimmings were ribbon sashes at the waist, ribbon bows on the drawstrings, rows of tucks around the hem, and an edging of lace at the neck.

In the early 1780s the waistline was worn in its natural place, and three drawstrings were the norm for chemise dresses, though the bottom one might be hidden by a broad sash. As the waistline rose in the 1790s the bottom drawstring was omitted, leaving the fullness to fall from just below the bust.

Two rare examples of this later type are at York Castle Museum, one of which is shown in Fig. 23. Both are of fine muslin, one plain and one checked, and both are embroidered in darning stitches. The bodices have groups of quarter-inch (0.6 cm) tucks across the front, indicating that this area may have been worn flat, not gathered. Both are completely open down the back seam. A

dress as flimsy as this would be for indoor use only; if worn outdoors it would be accompanied by pelisses similar to Fig. 15, shawls, and mittens (Fig. 24).

The silhouette of an adult woman of 1800 in evening dress was closer to that of a toddler of the period 1780–1790 than to that of a woman of 1770. The raised waistline, short sleeves, loose construction (concealing a hip-length corset) and lightweight fabrics were all attributes which related to children's clothes. The likeness was noted by contemporaries, who gave one type of women's bodice the name 'à l'enfant'.

Like the new styles of the 1920s, neo-classical dress was a superficially egalitarian fashion, favouring the young and slim over the old and wealthy. Status was judged by the fineness and whiteness of the muslin dress, and by the quality of the accessories, Indian shawls being particularly prized.

An example of the neo-classical style for girls is seen in Fig. 25. This dress of fine cotton was probably evening or 'best' wear. It is decorated with minute pintucks and white embroidery set on either side of an insertion of darned net. It is still open down the

Fig. 22   The Romps, William Redmore Bigg, 1790s. This painting shows how easily muslin chemise dresses could become dirty and disarranged. Several girls have coloured silk petticoats; all have broad ribbon sashes and coloured kid shoes. Some have plain turned-back sleeves, while others' sleeves are gathered in fashionable puffs.

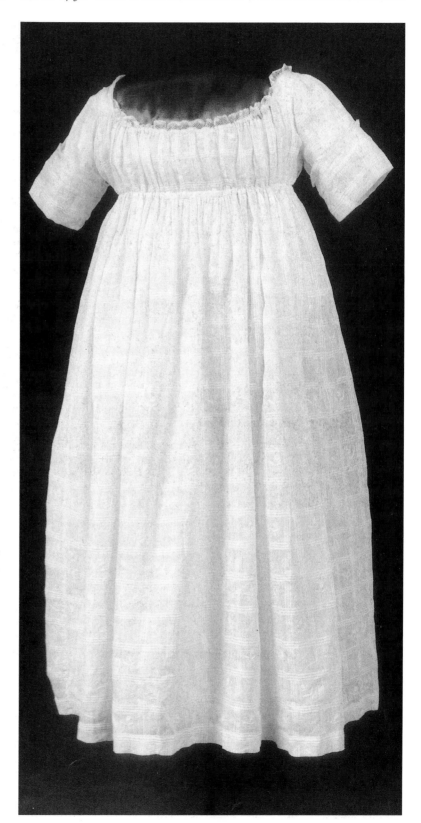

Fig. 23 An example of the gathered
muslin dresses of the 1790s. This one
has woven checks and embroidered
sprigs, probably worked at the time of
manufacture. The turned-back sleeves
derive from earlier styles. The back
seam is completely open, held by two
buttons and two drawstrings. Length
34.5 inches (87 cm).

back seam like eighteenth-century girls' dresses, but is provided with matching buttons. The slight train is to allow for a small bustle.

Other dresses of this period had no waistline at all, as can be seen in Joshua Johnson's portrait of Emma van Name, *c.* 1805.[13] Others had a strip of insertion outlining the 'bust' area, a feature adapted from women's dresses of about 1800, which sometimes had a very raised waistline which curved under the line of the breast.[14]

The traditional set of undergarments – chemise, stays and petticoat – would not be appropriate under a transparent and narrow dress such as Fig. 25. Various alternatives were tried in the years around 1800, including tubular petticoats of pink silk jersey and a form of tights made of the same material![15] The usual solution, however, was to wear drawers.

These might be made closed, with a back flap, like Fig. 35. They might also be made 'open', in which case the two legs were joined only at the waistband. Shoulder straps or bodices were popular when the waistline was at its highest. From the late 1820s the waist was at its natural level and the drawers were generally made open,

Fig. 24   The Sailor's Orphans, or The Young Ladies' Subscription, William Redmore Bigg (engraved by William Ward, 1799). This idealized scene contrasts young boarding-school pupils with an impoverished sailor's family. The girls' wear a variety of shawls, gloves and cloaks over their muslin dresses. The sailor's son wears a pair of striped trousers, presumably copied from his father's.

held in place by tight stays. Children's drawers were often trimmed with tucks and lace at the ankle, as they would be visible below the shortened skirts. Adults' drawers, too, were sometimes seen, though not intentionally.[16]

Not all cotton dresses were as fine as Fig. 25. By the early nineteenth century the mechanized cotton trade of Lancashire and Scotland had developed so much that cotton cloth was Britain's most valuable export. Much of this production was in the form of cheap printed fabrics, priced at a level which allowed working women to have several cotton dresses for the price of one woollen

Fig. 25 (above) A girl's formal dress, c. 1800, showing the high waist and flat front of the period. The fine muslin is trimmed with pintucks, white embroidery and lace insertion. Front length 40.5 inches (103 cm).

Fig. 26 A block-printed 'china-blue' cotton dress, c. 1810–20. It may have been made from a large scarf like the one in Fig. 21. The 'robings' on the skirt are a new feature. Length 21 inches (53 cm).

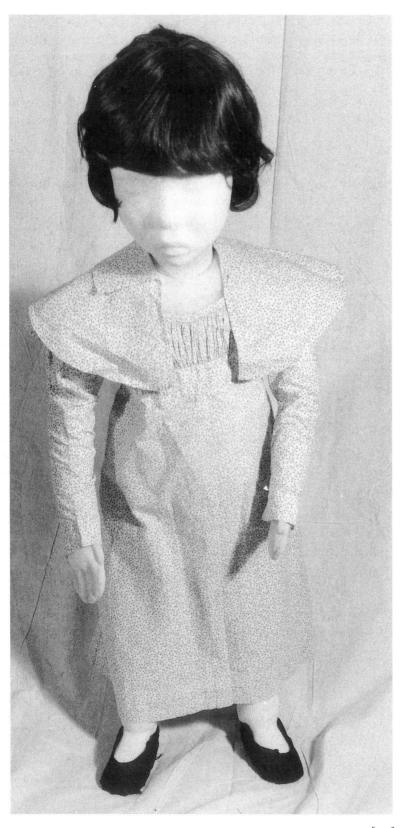

Fig. 27   A dress with matching tippet and sleeves, c. 1810–20. This example is printed in pink; its pair, in the same collection, is purple.

one.[17] An example of this cheaply made cotton can be seen in Fig. 26. This small girl's dress is made up from a piece of block-printed cotton which was probably intended for a large scarf or handkerchief. The scrolling border has been carefully used to decorate the hem, robings and bodice. Two of the corners have been kept to make the back bodice. The original handkerchief may have looked like the one tied around the girl playing blind-man's buff in Fig. 21.

Another printed cotton dress, Fig. 27, shows the delicate patterns produced by roller-printing. The shape of the dress itself is similar to Fig. 26 but in this case it has a pair of long sleeves and a small shoulder cape which can be tied on for use out of doors and in cold weather. Small capes called 'tippets' or short 'spencer' jackets were the accepted outdoor garments both for women and children in the early nineteenth century. Sometimes the cape and sleeves were attached to each other with strings, as in Fig. 65.

Between 1750 and 1820, girls' clothes had gone through a series of vast changes. These covered the material, cut and fit of their clothes and of their undergarments. Some of these changes were in response to adult fashion, such as the raising of the waistline from 1790 onwards. In other areas, such as the use of plain white linens and muslins for everyday wear, daughters were in advance of their mothers. It may be that the popularity of white dresses for young girls helped their acceptance by women in the 1780s. The changing adult silhouette, with less emphasis on a small waist, helped to spare young girls the miseries of tight stays – until adolescence, at least. Yet it was not a case of unmitigated gains. The new cotton dresses must have felt rather chilly by comparison with the old-fashioned layers of wool and silk. The narrow skirts of 1800 to 1820, were restrictive enough even without tubular petticoats. The plethora of strings and ties needed to attach extra sleeves and capes cannot have helped. However, the late eighteenth century had established simplicity and ease as the most appropriate criteria for childrens' clothes. These aims were often lost from sight as the nineteenth century progressed.

CHAPTER THREE

Boys: 1750-1820

In 1750, the young boy newly out of 'petticoats' was put into a miniature of adult dress. For the son of wealthy parents this would include a fitted silk coat and waistcoat, breeches, silk stockings and high-heeled shoes, a fine linen shirt trimmed with lace, and possibly even such non-essential accessories as a scaled-down sword, cane and powdered wig![1] The child of working parents would be dressed more simply, in a coat and breeches of wool or leather, a coarse wool or linen shirt, wool stockings, and strong leather shoes. In the early and mid eighteenth century a quasi-adult status appears to have been put on with adult styles of dress. In prints by Hogarth, children appear in the most notorious scenes of adult activity. This is particularly true of the young boys who are depicted as tavern servers or private servants in *The Rake's Wedding*, *Noon* and *The Election Supper*. While Hogarth may have pointed a moral by the contrast of youthful innocence and adult depravity, it is true that many children had to work for a living.

The picture presented by fashionable portraitists such as Slaughter is, understandably, rather different. In group portraits such as that of the children of Sir E. Walpole (Fig. 18) the children, although illegitimate, are shown as inheritors of their father's breeding and social status. Young Edward, aged 10, is portrayed in a silk velvet suit matched by a satin waistcoat, both trimmed with fancy buttons. Both stockings and shirt are of fine quality, and the waistcoat is left unbuttoned as much to display the shirt ruffle as for ease. The distinctions between his dress and that of a gentleman are few. He does not wear a cravat or neck-tie, though his shirt collar is fastened tightly. His hair is his own and in a style adapted from men's wigs. The more expensive accessories of male dress, such as watches, jewellery, and fine embroidery are also absent. Edward's childish status is demonstrated most clearly by his positioning within the group, linked to and dominated by his three sisters.

The fine, almost courtly clothes worn by Edward Walpole were not the only way for a gentleman's child to dress, however. The

The Bradshaw Family, *Johan Zoffany, 1769. The two boys wear suits adapted from men's country wear. The younger children (probably girls) have simple tucked linen dresses relieved by broad ribbon sashes and caps covered with lace.*

[45]

country-based existence of the large and small English gentry set them apart from their counterparts in France.[2] Simpler clothes were needed for a life of riding, hunting and superintending an estate. These sometimes appear in informal portraits, where the family is shown fishing or kite-flying in open parkland (Fig. 28). The boys' clothes in the Wheatley portrait group are cut more loosely than their father's, and are made of a lighter fabric, probably a linen mixture. Other signs of youth are their hair, now cut short and uncurled, and their open shirt collars.

A rare surviving example of a similar suit is shown in Figs. 29 and 30. It is made of dark brown linen, resist-printed with a circular pattern in rust-colour. The coat is cut like a man's, with shaped back seams. The fronts curve away to the hem, so that only two of the seven enamelled metal buttons can be used. The skirts have multiple back pleats and a deep vent to give freedom of movement. The breeches are cut like a man's with back fullness gathered into a band $2\frac{1}{2}$ inches (6·3 cm) deep which can be adjusted with laces at the back. The front opening is covered by a flap which buttons up at the right side. There is also a right hip pocket, again covered by a buttoned flap. These complex fastenings are typical of eighteenth-century breeches, and were retained in early versions of trousers. The knees of the breeches show a great deal of wear, and have been strengthened with cuffs of matching material. A more serious accident has struck the left sleeve of the coat,

Fig. 28   Family Group with a Negro Servant, Francis Wheatley, c. 1774. The two boys wear loose-fitting open-necked versions of their father's country suit. The toddler on their mother's knee has a simple muslin dress with tucks at the hem. The young girl wears a more fitted version of the same, with lace at the neck and on the cap. Her elder sister has graduated to a silk gown, through this is still back-fastening and is worn with a girlish bibbed apron.

Fig. 29   A young boy's suit of printed
linen, c. 1770–80. It has been well-worn
and patched, but still has its original
buttons of 'tortoiseshell' enamel. Coat
length 23.5 inches (59 cm).

Fig. 30   Breeches of the suit in Fig. 29,
showing the front flap and deep
waistband. The back split would be
closed with a lace. Length 16 inches
(40 cm).

where the bottom $4\frac{1}{2}$ inches ($11\cdot4\,$cm) have been replaced with a different fabric in the same weight and colours.

This type of suit, intended for and subjected to energetic use would have met with the wholehearted approval of the philosophers Locke and Rousseau. Both preferred country life and home tuition for boys as the best way to ensure 'a sound mind in a sound body'.[3] A country upbringing also offered an opportunity for the sons of the gentry to learn how to manage the landed estates which formed the greater part of their wealth. Rousseau would have been especially pleased by the classless appearance of Fig. 29; he disliked the French custom of punishing wealthy boys by making them wear 'peasant' clothing.[4]

During the 1760s and 1770s there were several attempts to find clothing suited to young boys just out of petticoats. One of these was the 'hussar' suit, based on the Hungarian military uniform, which was also a favourite for adult fancy dress. A striking example of a silk hussar suit can be seen in a portrait of the grandchildren of Empress Maria Theresa of Austria painted in 1778 by Johan Zoffany.[5] This suit differed from normal menswear in having a hip-length jacket fastened with decorative frogging. More importantly, it was worn with loose ankle-length trousers instead of breeches. Until this date trousers had been worn only by sailors and fishermen. It was the trousers that gave the hussar suit such a revolutionary appearance; they would be more comfortable to wear than kneebreeches, and would do away with the need for long stockings. However, these 'reformed' suits were soon being cut to fit as tightly as fashionable dress[6] and had only a limited popularity in Britain.

Other alternatives which met with a little more popularity in England were the loose suits consisting of a hip-length jacket and ankle-length trousers which are sometimes seen in English portraits of the 1760s and 1770s. One example is shown in a portrait of Wills Hill, Earl of Hillsborough and his family by Arthur Devis.[7] These, like the hussar suit, may have originated in masquerade costume. They appear to have been made of more decorative fabrics than a man's suit, and when worn with a downturned ruff collar are rather reminiscent of Watteau's portrait of Gilles, the famous pierrot.[8] As none of these 'pierrot' suits have survived it is difficult to say much about their fabric or construction, or to know how widely they were worn.

All of these attempts to redesign boys' clothing can be regarded as experimental. The majority of family portraits of the 1760s and 1770s show no transition between the white dress or slip worn up to the age of 4 or 5 and the miniature men's suits worn thereafter. However, in the 1780s a new outfit for boys appeared which was to prove influential throughout Europe, and which was firmly associated with English tastes and the English way of life. It had a loose waist-length jacket of dark wool or linen, either single or double-breasted, which was often worn open to show a pale-coloured waistcoat of cotton or linen. With it were worn the long

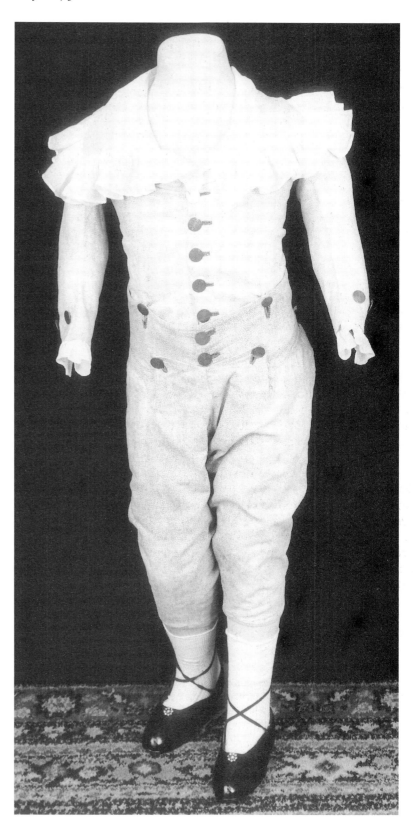

Fig. 31 An early skeleton suit c. 1780,
made of light-blue linen with flat metal
buttons. The ruffled shirt is made with
a wide collar. The trousers have the
deep waistband and fullness over the
seat of earlier breeches.

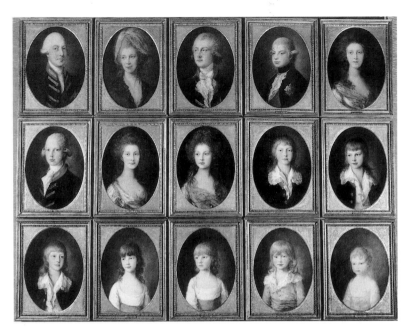

Fig. 32   The Royal Family, *Thomas Gainsborough, 1782. This group of portraits shows George III, Queen Charlotte, and 13 of their children starting with the Prince of Wales (George IV). The youngest child, Prince Alfred, was painted posthumously. The youngest still alive were Prince Octavius, age 3, and Princess Sophia, age 5.*

pantaloons of the hussar and pierrot suits, also in wool. These trousers were probably constructed like contemporary breeches, held up with a buttoned front band, laced at the back to control the fullness over the seat, and with a buttoned front flap.

Some paintings show these trousers with large buttons at the top of the side seams.[9] These may indicate a flap back, which would be an advantage with very small boys; but they could also be a decorative fastening for side pockets. The trousers were now cut to come high above the waist, unlike breeches, and young boys were given buttonholes to fasten them onto the bottom of the short jackets (Fig. 31). A lavish display of shirt collar and frilled edging was achieved by wearing the jacket and waistcoat open at the neck, with the collar turned back to the shoulders. This type of suit had a completely new silhouette which approached that of contemporary women, who were now wearing raised waistlines and frilled neckerchiefs.

The new suits were immediately and closely associated with England and with English attitudes to children. A version was illustrated in a German fashion magazine in 1787 with the caption 'comfortable and functional clothing for children based on the theories of John Locke'.[10] They were even adopted by the Royal children. King George III had a strong preference for both informality and uniformity in dress. When the Royal Family were painted by Gainsborough in 1782, the King himself and his three eldest sons were portrayed in the blue and red 'Windsor Uniform' he had devised. However, the next three sons, then aged from 11 to 8, were shown in new-style suits of the same fabric. The impression of informality is increased by the boys' natural, shoulder-length hair, and by the generous display of frilled collars (Fig. 32). In keeping with this informality, the two youngest princesses are dressed in plain white linen with silk sashes. Most interesting of all, the young Prince Octavius (aged 3) is wearing an early example of the 'skeleton suit', of strong linen or cotton. The slightly raised waistline is hidden by his sash. These suits became ubiquitous from the 1790s, and were even shown on prosperous rural children in paintings like Morland's *The Comforts of Industry*, 1790.[11] But they were still seen as a half-way house between babyhood and young manhood. Older boys would progress into a tail-coat cut like a man's, matching or contrasting breeches and waistcoat and white stockings. The only concessions to youth were the long hair and the open-necked shirt. The contrast between older and younger boys can be seen in W. R. Bigg's painting of 1800 (Fig. 33). Here the older boys wear both breeches and trousers while the younger boys are all in skeleton suits.

Even when the suits were made of washable fabrics like linen cleanliness was still a problem, exacerbated by their light colours and tight fit. Men's drawers were still an optional garment, with voluminous thigh-length shirts often providing the only layer between body and suit lining. Such large shirts could not be worn beneath the tight trousers, and their place was taken by narrow-cut trousers or by detachable 'linings' sewn into the trousers. The frills of the shirt collar were also a status symbol, requiring careful washing and ironing.

By 1800, some variants had appeared in the standard skeleton suit. One was to make the jacket in a dark-coloured wool, and the trousers in white or natural cotton or linen (Fig. 63).[12] This strong

Fig. 33 The Soldier's Widow, or The Schoolboys' Collection, *William Redmore Bigg, 1800 (engraved by Robert Dunkarton, 1802). This painting shows the variety of clothes worn by boys of different ages, from skeleton suits to jacket and breeches. Interestingly, one of the senior boys wears close-fitting trousers. The soldier's young daughter has what looks like a cut-down uniform jacket.*

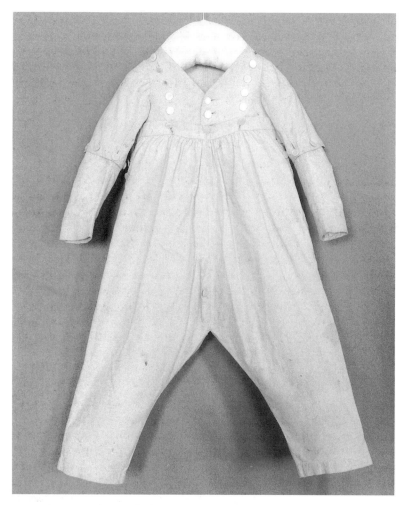

Fig. 34 (left) A variant on the skeleton suit for a young boy, c. 1800–10, made of buff coloured cotton-linen fabric trimmed with mother-of-pearl buttons. The trousers button round the waist and down the sides, with a falling back. A ruffled shirt would be worn under this suit. Length 27 inches (69 cm).

Fig. 35 (below) A young boy's 'jumpsuit' of buff cotton with matching embroidery, c. 1822. Back view, showing the fastenings. The eyelet embroidery anticipates mid nineteenth-century broderie anglaise (see Chapter 4). Length 26.5 inches (67 cm).

contrast was also in fashion for women, who wore dark-coloured spencer jackets over their light muslin dresses.[13] Very young boys' jackets might be made with short sleeves, or with long sleeves buttoned onto short (Fig. 34). This feature may have been intended to save wear on cuffs, or it may have been a reaction to the fashion for 'nudity' in women's dress.

It seems that by 1800 boys were being 'breeched' at an earlier age than they had been in mid-century. There is certainly a plethora of garments from this date which were designed for the needs of the 2 to 4-year-old. One such is the modified skeleton suit shown in Fig. 34. Its very high waist and narrow shoulders reflect female fashions, as does the gathered fullness of the trousers. These are not made like earlier trousers or breeches but more like the new under-drawers. The $4\frac{1}{2}$ inch (11.4 cm) slit in the side seam allows the back to be let down for greater convenience, and there is also a front fly closed with a buttoned flap. The flat buttons trimming the outfit were a favourite feature of small boys' clothes; these are of mother-of-pearl, but brass was also used.

The back-flap opening is also used on an unusual 'jumpsuit' of

Fig. 36 A young boy's tunic and trousers of heavy cotton with feather-stitch embroidery, c. 1810–20. The trousers are made like those in Fig. 34. Tucks have been let down at the hem of the trousers but not on the tunic. Tunic length 24 inches (60 cm).

about 1822 (Fig. 35). This all-in-one outfit acted as a transition between dress and trousered suit. The cut is very similar to that used for children's underwear,[14] though the material and decoration make it clear that this is an outer garment. The bodice, with an embroidered front panel and frilled 'robings', is based on a toddler's dress. The trousers are gathered to a high waist as in Fig. 34, but are attached to the bodice at the front. The back flap is held in place by the belt of the bodice, and by the buttons of the side slit. Suits of this type appear occasionally in paintings around 1815,[15] but probably enjoyed only limited popularity as only three examples survive, Fig. 35 and two others in the collections of the National Museum of Scotland and the Museum of Costume, Bath.

For parents who preferred a more gradual change from babyhood to boyhood, trousers similar to those in Fig. 34 could be worn under a shortened dress. The most distinctive feature of these dresses was the slit from waist to hem which allowed the trousers to be seen (Fig. 36). They also tended to be made of coarser and plainer fabric than girls' dresses – natural calico was a frequent choice. The example in Fig. 36 looks rather oddly proportioned because the tucks which allowed for growth have been let out on the trousers but not on the tunic! Usually the tunic was calf length.

The small boy of 1820 had apparently gained a great deal when contrasted with his bewigged, silk-suited ancestors. The light-coloured, close-fitting skeleton suits echoed the contemporary preference for 'natural' and semi-nude effects. Yet, as Rousseau had warned, the gains of the new style were more apparent than real. The cotton and linen fabrics chosen for the new-style suits were colder than silk and wool, had less 'give' in wear, and soiled much more easily. The obsession with a form-fitting cut, when combined with the very high waistline of the early nineteenth century, resulted in the discomforts described by Dickens:

> a skeleton suit, one of those straight blue cloth cases in which small boys used to be confined ... [giving] his legs the appearance of being hooked on just under the armpits.[16]

CHAPTER FOUR

Babies: 1820-1890

Clothes for women, children and infants were very different in 1820 from those of 70 years previously. A natural figure was the ideal, without excessively tight corsets. This was to be shown off in unprecedentedly revealing dresses with low necks, short sleeves and narrow skirts. Favoured fabrics were now fine muslins and printed cottons rather than stiff silks and linens. For formal occasions these would be enlivened with lace, net and gauze.

Infants had benefitted more directly from changes in childrearing practice than from general fashion trends. Foremost among these was the gradual abandonment of swaddling. By the early nineteenth century, the only reminder of it was the 'binder' or 'roller', a strip of flannel or stout cotton three or four inches (7.5–10 cm) wide, which was wound around an infant's midriff several times before being pinned onto itself. This was used to flatten the navel and support the lower back and stomach. Rollers were still in use in the early twentieth century.[1]

In all other respects, early nineteenth-century infants seem to have suffered from rather too much freedom. Extremely low-cut and short-sleeved dresses were the norm for daywear, though long sleeves were allowed on nightdresses and newborns' monthly gowns. As with older children, the effects of such skimpy garments would be mitigated by tie-on sleeves for indoors, and by shawls or capes for outdoors. The relative simplicity of the basic dress was also compensated for by the increasing elaboration of its trimmings and accessories.

By 1820 the standard gown (Fig. 37) had a very low square neck, a shallow bodice as little as two inches (5 cm) deep, extremely short sleeves sometimes cut in two overlapping 'petals' or made up of segmented puffs, and a gathered skirt up to 40 inches (101 cm) long (*The Workwoman's Guide* in 1840 recommended a length of 40 inches for children of the 'rich', and 34 inches (86 cm) for the 'poor').[2] This would be worn over several cotton petticoats, a linen shirt, and quilted or corded stays (Fig. 45).

The general proportions of these gowns were based on women's evening dress. There were, however, some differences of detail;

This babygown, c. 1875, shows a lavish use of machine-worked 'Swiss' embroidery, offset with panels of fine hand tucking and gathering. The joins are concealed by lines of feather-stitch.

one was the practice of tying up the sleeves with ribbons so that they fell off the shoulder. Another was the 'robings' which framed the front panel of the bodice and skirt (Fig. 37). They appear occasionally on women's dresses of the 1820s and afterwards, but only as fashion dictated. Yet they remained an essential part of babies' gowns until the 1890s. Early versions were perpendicular and widely spaced, like the tucks in some late eighteenth-century muslin dresses. By the 1830s they were placed so as to form two triangular panels reminiscent of the decorated stomacher and petticoat front of eighteenth-century women's dress. Even the plainest babygowns would usually have some kind of decorative finish on the robings (Fig. 38).

Fig. 37   Queen Victoria as an Infant, J. P. G. Fischer, 1819. The young princess wears a simple cotton dress. Like others of the same date, it has a very shallow bodice and widely spaced robings trimmed with tucks. The sleeves are tied up with ribbon. The only signs of status are the lace edging on the cap and the cashmere shawl used as a coverlet.

Fig. 38   A plain babygown of the 1820s. The horizontal tucks and buttons are reminiscent of boys' hussar tunics (see Fig. 65) while the sleeves are copied from a woman's evening dress. The bodice panel has been lengthened, either to fit a growing child or to follow changing fashions.

Fig. 39   A very fine Ayrshire work babygown, presented to Mrs Jamieson by her workwomen on the birth of her grandchild in 1851. It is supposed to be a copy of one made by the firm for the birth of the Prince of Wales in 1841. All the flowers have needlelace fillings.

The finest quality gowns were those produced by the Ayrshire needlework industry. This had been founded by Mrs Jamieson of Ayr in 1814[3] (Fig. 39). She took advantage of the cotton mills in the area of Glasgow and Edinburgh (both great ports, and having the moist climate needed for cotton spinning), and of the abundance of skilled female labour in the surrounding countryside. The women were organized into groups, working in their own homes under a 'putter-out', and produced fine work following the patterns provided by the manufacturers. These patterns were of the highest standard of design (fostered by new Academies of Design in Glasgow and Edinburgh) the better to appeal to fashionable tastes. However, the lasting popularity of the 'flowered' work derived from the very high quality of the embroidery. The fine evenweave muslins and cambrics produced in Scotland in the early nineteenth century enabled the workers to use a very tight, almost raised satin-stitch for the bulk of the design.

The firmer fabric also permitted the lavish use of insertions. These were not of the bobbin lace or hollie point favoured in the eighteenth century, but of a great variety of needle fillings. They differed from hollie point in being less densely worked, and less based on a grid. The needle fillings were one of the chief novelties of Ayrshire work, and their extent determined the price of the finished piece. The finished areas were still small, because of the fragility and cost of the work.

The needle fillings were the responsibility of specialists who were more highly paid than the other workers.[4] 'Assembly line' methods were applied throughout the Ayrshire work industry, and were one of the chief reasons for its consistently high standards. One woman might be responsible for the simple edgings, another for the more elaborate motifs; a specialist would work the needle fillings and a seamstress would make up the finished piece. The work might be sold to the customer at several stages of manufacture; it was possible to buy pieces with the centre of the motifs left blank for the purchaser to add her own filling or net insertion (Fig. 40). It is also very common to find babygowns where the edgings do not match the embroidered panels, suggesting that these were bought separately. Especially fine skirt and bodice panels and cap crowns were often reused in larger or newer garments. One type of babygown, where the embroidery on the skirt tapers off 18 inches (46 cm) above the hem, seems to have been designed for remodelling; the skirt panel would be just the right size for converting into a toddler's dress. This adaptability was another point in favour of the Ayrshire productions.

Another technique which was used for baby clothes in the 1820s was embroidered net. Machine-made net fabric was a novelty which had been patented by John Heathcoat in 1808.[5] Previously, plain net had been made by hand using lacemaking techniques which made it prohibitively expensive. Machine-made net was a luxury fabric which could be darned to imitate lace, or embroidered with Ayrshire-type motifs. It was generally restricted to

Fig. 40 The front panel of an Ayrshire work gown of the 1830s. Although the gown is complete, the space for the needle fillings have been left blank. Peacocks were a favourite motif on babygowns produced in the Glasgow area, while the floral sprays relate to contemporary shawl designs.

small pieces such as women's collars and sleeves and babies' caps (Fig. 42). Small pieces of net with darned patterns sometimes replace needle fillings in Ayrshire work gowns; but these may be repairs, not original. Net was occasionally used for toddlers' best dresses; these were trimmed with bands of silk satin and worn over a satin underdress.

At the other end of the social scale babies were dressed much more simply, with printed cotton or flannel gowns cut like wealthier babies' nightgowns. These were made in one piece, with a high neck and long sleeves. The fullness of the skirts was held in by ties or drawstrings attached to either end of a band sewn over the front waist. *The Workwoman's Guide* comments on these day and nightgowns:

> This shape is the one generally used by the lower classes, not only for flannels, but for print gowns and petticoats; and is preferred to others on account of the ease with which it is cut out, and also because there is much less needle-work in the making.[6]

These simple gowns were in use throughout the nineteenth century and into the twentieth, far outnumbering the elaborate creations shown in fashion magazines (Fig. 58).

In the late 1820s and early 1830s infants' and women's dresses were at their closest in terms of outline, material and trimming.

Fig. 41   Three babycaps of the early 1830s, with extravagant lace ruffles and a wealth of needle fillings.

Fig. 42   The crown of an embroidered net babycap, c. 1840. The embroidery is similar in design and technique to Ayrshire work; the centre of the flower has a darned filling. The embroidery would probably be worked over a tissue paper backing.

The new 'hourglass' silhouette was reflected in the triangular front panels of babygowns. The wide ruffled robings on the bodice and around the neck of babies' dresses corresponded to the broad shoulders and full sleeves of their mothers. Plain white muslin was now going out of fashion for adults, but it was still very much in demand for accessories such as wide collars and extravagantly frilled caps for both mother and infant (Fig. 41).

All of these were frequently executed in Ayrshire needlework, and by the same manufacturers who were turning out baby gowns in their thousands. The same exuberant motifs of stylized flowers and curled sprays can be found on both, though the fillings may be slightly less elaborate and extensive on adult garments. Similar motifs were also used for the new darned net lace and for the shawls produced at Paisley and at Norwich.

By 1840, the fashion in adults' clothing was making a decisive change back to heavier, closer-fitting, and darker-coloured garments. The area of exposed whitework contracted sharply to a straight collar a few inches wide and a narrow cuff. Caps, when worn, fitted the head closely with no exuberant frills. Petticoats might still have embroidered hems, but these were only rarely visible beneath skirts which touched the foot.

These changes left the Ayrshire work industry more dependent than before on infants' garments, and on lengths of trimming which could be made up at home. The baby gowns of the 1840s and early 1850s show an undiminished quality of design, with needlefilled fruit and flowers set amid scrolling tendrils (Fig. 43). The needlefillings are, however, increasingly supplemented with large areas of pulled thread work. The regular grids of these areas are rather out of character with the rest of the embroidery.

Richly coloured wool and cashmere fabrics returned to fashion in the 1840s after decades of being regarded as second best compared to muslins and printed cottons. It was a reaction to adult fashions which brought wool back into favour for infants' clothes. Wool had been used since the eighteenth century for flannel vests and petticoats[7] but not for outer garments. Curiously, one type of flannel petticoat which was popular throughout the nineteenth century was made like an eighteenth-century 'slip' gown, from a large piece of fabric pleated into shape.[8]

By 1840 it was usual for babies' cloaks to be made from fine wool or cashmere cloth. These were made as much as 40 inches (101 cm) long and six feet (1.8 m) around the hem, with capes and collars for extra warmth. All this fabric hung from a single ribbon tie round the baby's neck. The favourite colours for baby capes were dull, like those used for women's cloaks: fawn, grey and muted purple. They might be decorated with broad silk facings, or with patterns of interlaced braid. These garments could be made at home, using patterns from needlework books such as *The Work-woman's Guide*,[9] or from women's magazines. They were, however, increasingly bought ready-made from one of the large drapery and fancy-goods warehouses established in London and

Fig. 43 The skirt panel of an Ayrshire work babygown, c. 1850. An exceptionally rich effect is given by the combination of swirling satin-stitch tendrils, extensive needle fillings and areas of pulled-thread work. The border at the foot of the panel was a poplar feature in the 1840s.

provincial towns. One Oxford Street warehouse was selling babies' cashmere cloaks at prices ranging from 12s. to £4.4s. in 1856; yet the needlewomen who made them in their own homes were paid as little as 8d. for up to 14 hours work![10]

Wool fabrics were also used for toddlers' dresses in the 1840s. These were usually made very simply, with a plain bodice, long sleeves, and a full pleated skirt. They might also have a matching shoulder cape so that they could be worn outdoors without a coat (Colour Plate 3). Printed or woven checks were often chosen for these dresses as patterns which needed no additional decoration and which showed up well on the full skirts. Checked woollens also alluded to the Royal Family's fascination with Scotland, which had a great influence on young boys' clothes (see Chapter 6).

By the late 1850s, the rather restrained taste of the 1840s had been transformed into a desire for outright display. Women's dresses were now up to four yards (3.7 m) in circumference, with their apparent bulk increased by layers of flounces. New inventions such as the sewing machine and synthetic dyes helped to create fashions which were anything but retiring. The great expanse of fashionable dresses required trimmings which were larger and bolder than delicate Ayrshire work. This need was supplied by 'broderie anglaise' embroidery which consisted of groups of different shaped eyelets arranged in bold patterns of flowers and swirls (Fig. 44). It quickly found favour for toddlers' dresses, and for the front panels and edgings of babygowns.

Its popularity rested partly on its greater durability and resistance to washing when compared to Ayrshire work, and partly on the ease and speed with which it could be worked. Children's dresses, drawers and petticoats made from broderie anglaise could be bought ready made, or made up at home from purchased lengths and panels. The embroidery itself could also be worked at home, as it needed more patience than skill. Pieces of fabric could be bought with the pattern of a collar and cuffs, or a child's bodice front, stamped on them.

Its popularity extended throughout the British Empire; by the late nineteenth century native embroiderers in India had assimilated the style and were producing baby gowns and even adult dresses for the families of expatriate Europeans.[11] These can usually be recognized by the angular, rather exotic motifs with spindly, rather thinly worked tendrils, and most importantly, by the presence of 'hali' or 'jali' stitch. This is a pulled-work stitch traditional to Northern India, which gives a checked openwork effect.

In spite of competition from cheaper types of embroidery, Ayrshire work maintained its place at the upper end of the market. A government survey of 1857 found it in a very healthy state, with a wages bill of £80,000 per annum.[12] Yet during the 1860s this flourishing industry was almost completely destroyed by two sets of events. The first was the American Civil War of 1861–4, which

Fig. 44   A small child's dress of broderie anglaise, 1860s. The bold effects produced by this technique were ideally suited to the showy fashions of the late 1850s and 1860s. A ribbon sash was usually worn on the shoulder by a boy, round the waist by a girl. Length 24 inches (61 cm).

caused a break in Britain's imports of raw cotton. The shortage of the raw material caused lengthy stoppages in the cotton mills of Lancashire and Scotland, and a great fall in production. The other outside factor was the development of machine embroidery by firms based in Switzerland. This work was being exported from Switzerland in the 1850s, and by the 1880s it had become the standard form of decoration for cheaper items such as petticoats.[13]

It is much easier to speak about late nineteenth-century babies' and children's clothes than it is for earlier periods. This is partly because more examples survive, sometimes in sets of 'a dozen of everything'. There also fuller written and pictorial sources available for the period, including photographs and popular women's magazines. Chief among these was the *Englishwoman's Domestic Magazine*, edited by Samuel Beeton and his wife Isabella. Unlike some earlier publications it was aimed at a family audience, and concentrated on household hints and current affairs rather than fashion and romance.

Another publication catering for the same readership was *Cassell's Household Guide* which first appeared in 1868. Its four volumes include lengthy articles on childrearing and instructions for making infants' and children's clothing at home. It gives the standard outfit for a newborn baby as: a fine linen shirt, open down the back, made with flaps to turn down over the top of the binder or petticoat; a long 'day-flannel' or 'blanket', still shaped with pleats like the version of 1840; one or more long cotton petticoats with either a fitted or a wrap-around bodice; and finally a cotton day gown about 36 inches (90 cm) long in the skirt.

Below this were worn a square nappy of either figured linen or cotton towelling, a flannel 'pilch' and possibly a pair of hand-knitted socks. It was now recognized that newborns needed more warmth, and the pattern given for a 'first sized' or monthly gown stipulates long sleeves and a high neck, similar to those recommended for a nightgown. Another new feature was the use of hand or machine quilting to hold down the pleats of the flannel petticoat bodice. Quilting was also recommended for stiffening the stays

Fig. 45 A baby's corded cotton stays, mid nineteenth-century. Corded stays were worn by both sexes for their first few years. Boys left them off when they put on their first masculine suit, but girls continued in longer and stiffer versions until they graduated to a fully boned corset.

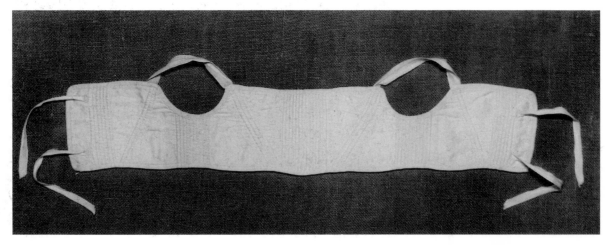

Fig. 46   A babygown with a tucked
front panel, 1870s. This dress shows
the influence of mechanization in both
the machine-sewn tucks and the 'Swiss
embroidered' insertions and edgings. A
panel made up of tucks and insertions
was the most common choice for
babydresses in the 1870s and 1880s.

worn by older babies and toddlers (Fig. 45), and for the uppers of silk indoor shoes (Fig. 48).

The patterns in *Cassell's* are interesting for the insight they give into the domestic life of the middle-class families for whom the book was intended. Most of the styles illustrated are the same as those found in surviving examples, showing that the authors judged the taste of their readers correctly. This is particularly true of the dresses with tucked 'princess' front panels (Fig. 46). These were particularly easy to make on the new sewing machine, which was available in domestic sizes from the mid-1850s onwards.[14]

The tucked-front gown remained popular into the 1890s, and innumerable variants survive. Many are decorated with frills or insertions of 'Swiss' machine embroidery between the tucks. The number of the surviving gowns, and the somewhat mechanical pattern to which they are made, suggests that they were mass-produced by wholesale drapers.

Another garment described in *Cassell's* which corresponds closely to surviving examples is the two-tier carrying cloak or cape. These were used when taking the baby outside for its airing, and would show up well when draped over the nurse's arms. *Cassell's* explains how to make a pattern by drawing a series of half-circles on sheets of newspaper, and how to make up and trim the cloak. The suggested colour schemes are bold, unlike the subtle shades used in the 1840s; bright blue or red with white facings. The facings could be quilted by hand, or made up from ready-quilted silk. Fig. 47 shows a carrying cape almost identical to those illustrated in *Cassell's*, worn with a machine-quilted silk hood.

When it comes to older children, *Cassell's* assumes that little boys will wear dresses or tunics up to the age of 8! This is a striking reversal of the practice earlier in the century, when boys would be put into skeleton suits as young as 2 or 4.[15] Not surprisingly, the later age of 'breeching' required a greater variety of distinctive boys' dresses:

> Boy's bodies are always cut straight at the waist, and not sloped. They may have a single tuck in the skirt to let down, but are not made with fancy tucks. Neither are the skirts or bodies trimmed in any way unless with a welt straight down the front and large buttons in it, or a slanting trimming brought from the left shoulder in an oblique line.[16]

These are discussed more fully in Chapter 6.

For everyday wear, children's dresses were made of wool, wool mixture, or cotton piqué, according to the season. Toddlers' dresses were usually made very simply, with a plain bodice and a skirt pleated into the waist, and trimmed with bands of black velvet or braided patterns according to the material. Indoor dresses were generally made with short puffed sleeves, but for outdoor wear the long-sleeved 'pelisse' with matching cape was thought more appropriate. These pelisses, looking very like those in Colour Plate 3, were a dual-purpose garment: 'In very cold

Fig. 47 A baby's carrying cape of deep-blue wool trimmed with quilted white silk and tassels, c. 1870. This could have been made at home; the separate hood, of machine-quilted silk with feather trimming, was probably mass-produced.

weather it is put over the frock, or frock and pinafore; in warmer weather the frock is removed.[17]

A similar practicality is seen in the pinafore, which had become more elaborate, with box-pleats and braided trimming. These more decorative pinafores could also be worn instead of a dress, saving wear and tear on more expensive garments. In all of these garments, the influence of adult fashion was seen mainly in the width of the skirts; 'A skirt for a child of two should not measure less than two yards round. Often three yards is allowed.'[18]

The choice of materials was also guided by fashion; rich-coloured wool trimmed with black velvet had been used for women's dresses in the late 1860s, and braided piqué was a favourite for summer and seaside dresses. On the whole, however, toddlers' everyday clothes show remarkably few changes from the late 1840s through to the late 1870s. Their simplicity of cut meant that they could easily be made up at home, and encouraged a democracy of appearance. Versions of the dresses and pinafores described by *Cassell's* can be seen in paintings of cottage interiors of the mid nineteenth century, made up in hardwearing serge, cotton print and 'holland' (Fig. 58).

The underwear worn by young children in the late 1870s was similar to that required in the 1840s, but with an even greater reliance on wool. A flannel chemise or vest would be worn next to the skin, then corded stays, cotton drawers, a flannel petticoat and one or more cotton petticoats trimmed with tucks or 'Swiss' embroidery. As a concession to childhood, the drawers were made with a drop seat and buttoned onto an underbodice. This anticipated the 'combinations' which were introduced in the 1880s, replacing a separate chemise and drawers.

From the mid-1840s to the late 1860s the distinguishing feature of women's fashion had been extremely full skirts, usually supported by stiffened petticoats or by a wire 'cage' crinoline.

Fig. 48   Three pairs of decorated children's shoes from the nineteenth century. The pair on the left are maroon kid embroidered with silk, c. 1840. The central pair, with original box, were made for Queen Victoria's Jubilee in 1887. 'Queen' and a crown are embroidered in metallic beads on the toes. The third pair are a baby's first shoes, made of quilted blue silk. Instructions for making similar shoes are given in Cassell's, *1868.*

Fig. 49   A child's dress of the 1880s, in natural linen with red 'Swiss embroidered' trimming. Simply shaped, with pleats in the back skirt and a sailor collar, this dress may be a later development of mid nineteenth-century 'overall' pinafores which could be worn over a dress, or instead of one.

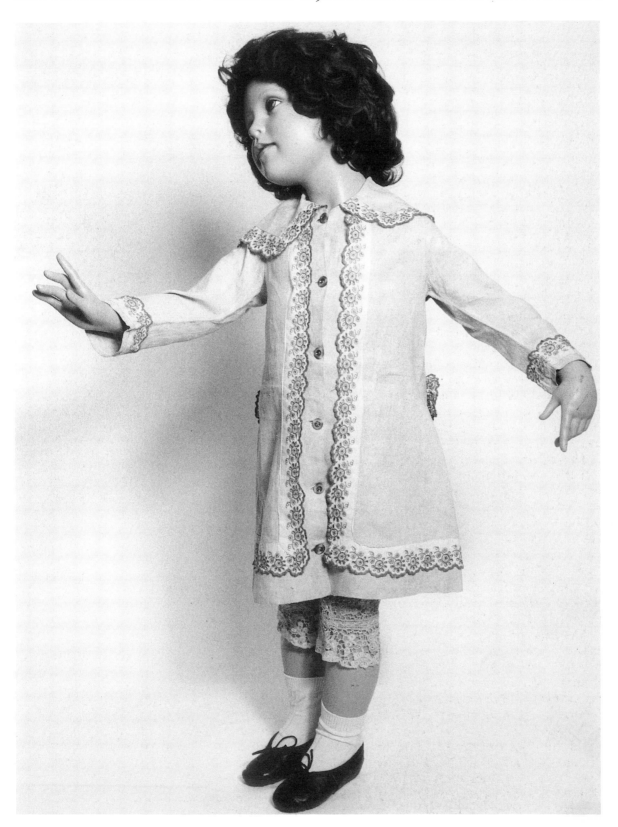

Fig. 50   A small child's dress of c. 1885, in cream wool with silk embroidery. The smocked and ruched panels are applied to a fitted lining, as in Fig. 61. This shape was also recommended for boys up to 6 years old!

Suddenly, in the mid-1870s, this fullness disappeared and by the late 1870s fashionable women were finding it difficult to walk in their narrow-skirted dresses! These new dresses were usually cut in one piece, without a waist seam, and were often decorated with a vertical panel in a contrasting texture, running from neck to hem.

The new styles had a limited influence on babywear. Baby gowns were made as full and as waisted as ever, though the panel of tucks might be *en princesse* (with no waist seam). They did, however, affect the cut of toddlers' dresses, which were no longer made with separate bodice and skirt. The fashionable shapes were either a simple A-line, with a minimum of waist shaping, or a bloused, low-waisted bodice and short pleated skirt (Figs 49 and 50). The first of these shapes, the A-line, was often made front-opening and long-sleeved, with large decorative buttons. The coat-like details suggest that these may have been used like the earlier pelisses. The second shape, with a clearly defined skirt, was more popular from 1885 onwards, as it could be adapted to the bustled profile of high fashion. In spite of their feminine appearance, dresses like Fig. 50 were worn as tunics by boys up to 6 years old. A dressmaking magazine of 1886 illustrates a similar example with the description: 'This pretty little tunic is made with plain and embroidered velvet. The edge of the tunic is cut in tabs, each one embroidered.'[19]

In many ways the picture presented by nineteenth-century babywear is one of extreme stability. The types of garment worn, and their cut, were established by the 1830s and remained unchanged in essentials until the 1890s. Toddlers' clothes show more variation, but most of this comes either before or after the central period 1840–80. Towards the end of the century the rate of change accelerated, spurred on by new inventions which included the safety pin (1849).[20]

CHAPTER FIVE

Girls: 1820-1890

By 1820, the first flush of neo-classicism in dress had burnt itself out, and had been replaced by romanticism; details of dress such as neck ruffs, 'Vandyke' edgings and hussar braiding were borrowed from the Gothic past, or from contemporary but exotic cultures. Both the fabrics and the silhouette of fashion had altered subtly since 1800; the shape was less tubular, the skirts were shorter and wider with flounced hems, and the waist was gradually growing tighter and lower. Sleeves grew fuller at the top until by 1830 they were full-blown gigots (leg-of-mutton sleeves), only subsiding in the early 1840s. The relatively extravagant use of fabric was matched by a taste for luxurious materials.

Fine muslin had been overthrown for evening wear by the new 'patent net' and by silk blonde lace. Printed cottons were still fashionable for daytime, but were now printed with boldly figured stripes or diagonals rather than the small-scale spots and sprigs of 1800–15. The effect was further brightened by a lavish use of whitework embroidery in double caped collars and long 'pelerines', cuffs and frilled indoor caps. These accessories do not survive in children's sizes, nor are children shown wearing them in portraits. They were probably too expensive and too easily soiled for children's wear.

Girls' white dresses, in the 1820s and 1830s, were kept exclusively for 'best' wear (Fig. 51). Made of fine cambric decorated with hand embroidery or lace insertion, they were styled after women's evening dresses, with low necks, short and fashionably cut sleeves, and full skirts. The fashion for coloured silk under-dresses to show off the transparency of the muslin or net above died out in the 1820s, to be revived in the 1870s.

These dresses were worn with several tightly gathered petticoats, drawers (sometimes attached to a bodice), a chemise, and some form of stays (Figs 52 and 53). Stays resumed their place in girls' upbringing as the fashionable waist grew lower and smaller, reaching wasp-like dimensions by the 1840s. With off-the-shoulder dresses, the straps of the stays would be worn over the upper arm.

Terracotta satin dress, c. 1885. A one-piece dress with a two-piece effect, modelled on a late eighteenth-century man's coat. Made as a sample for Marshall and Snelgrove, London.

[73]

Fig. 51 (left)   Girl's dress of white
cotton with net insertions, c. 1830. Net
was still enough of a novelty to be used
on its own, like lace. The elaborate
puffed sleeves are taken from adult
fashion. Length 32 inches (81 cm).

Fig. 52 (right)   Girl's drawers with a
shallow bodice, c. 1820 (also shown in
Fig. 51). Cotton with muslin frills.
Early drawers were often made with a
bodice to keep them in place under
very high-waisted dresses. The
decorated ankles would show beneath
a short dress. Length 34 inches (86 cm).

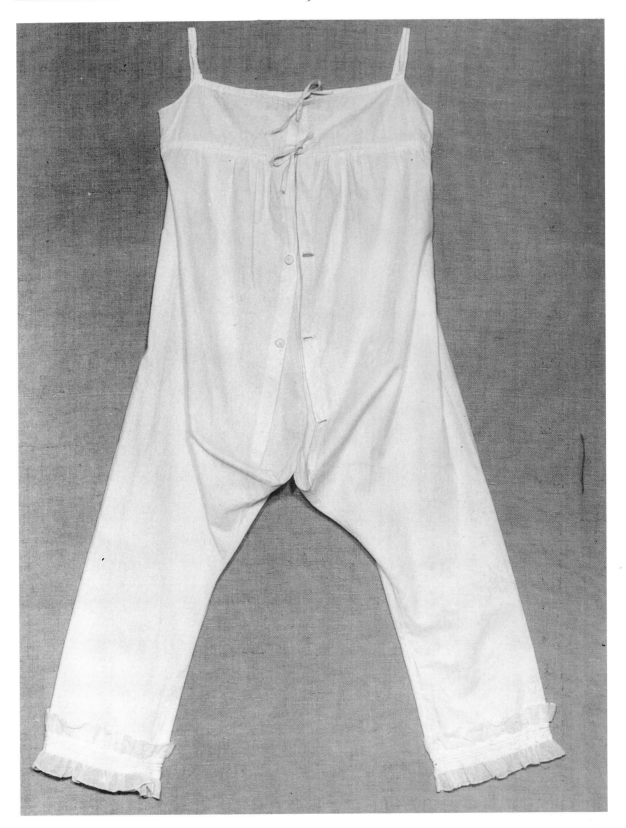

This ensured ladylike behaviour by preventing the wearer from raising her arms.

Less formal dresses were generally made of printed cotton or cotton-mixtures in varying weights. Heavier fabrics such as wool or velvet were occasionally used in winter, but these survive only in written records and may have been considered second best and unfashionable.

For warmth out of doors, girls might still wear the spencers which had been fashionable since the 1790s, either matching or contrasting with the dress. The small triangular shawls seen in Fig. 24 were now worn only by poorer people. The fashionable alternatives were a shaped triangular tippet, with or without sleeves attached, or a pelisse.

Pelisses were originally coats made of dark coloured silk, cut like a dress but open down the front, and sometimes wadded with lambswool for extra warmth. The pelisse-robe was a forerunner of the modern 'coat-dress'; it looked like a pelisse, but opened only to the knee, and would be worn with a hat and muslin accessories for visiting or shopping.[1] In the 1830s pelisses were also made in light-weight cottons for summer wear, and these are often so elaborate as to be barely distinguishable from dresses.

A small-scale pelisse in pink sprigged cotton, now in Bethnal Green Museum, was made for a girl called Henrietta Byron in 1840 (Fig. 54). The edges and pocketholes are trimmed with narrow

Fig. 53 (left)   *Girl's cotton stays with slots for whalebone at front and back, c. 1830–50. Made up of shaped pieces, stiffened with cording. Chest 29.5 inches (75 cm)*

Fig. 54 (right)   *A pelisse of pink printed cotton edged with white embroidery, c. 1840. It has a matching tippet. The 'robings' on the skirt occasionally appeared on adult dresses in the 1830s and 1840s. The decorated pockets are an unusual feature.*

*Fig. 55   A dress of red and blue silk
tartan worn by Victoria, Princess
Royal, eldest daughter of Queen
Victoria, at the age of 10 in 1850. The
'waistcoat' effect of white muslin is
unusual.*

white embroidery and feather stitching, and the button fastenings are concealed by bows. There is a matching tippet which fits under the collar. This garment is part of a set which were probably made for a girl being sent away to school, as they are all marked with her name and the date. If so, the wearer was probably about 8 years old. The set also has a long-sleeved velvet spencer, but Fig. 54 is the only coat; perhaps it was intended as a pelisse-robe, to be worn on its own in warmer weather. As a comment on Henrietta's newly grown-up status, the set includes a set of stays, stiffened with cords and gored at the bust.

By the mid-1840s female fashions had become more restrictive and even oppressive, with tight bodices, long, narrow sleeves and full skirts reaching to the feet. The effect of heaviness was increased by a change in fashionable fabrics; for the first time wool and wool-mixtures were fashionable in their own right, and not only as a concession to the British climate. This was prompted by improvements in dyeing technology which allowed wool to be printed with elaborate checks in intense blues and violets formerly reserved for linens, silks and cottons.

Wool also featured largely in girls' underwear, in the form of flannel vests or chemises, flannel petticoats and long wool stockings. Red flannel petticoats were supposed to be especially healthy, and were often worn under the wide skirts of the 1850s and 1860s. The layers of wool were usually worn in addition to a standard set of cotton underclothes, making girls' clothes even heavier and tighter!

The type of fabric most associated with mid nineteenth-century Britain is tartan. It owed its popularity to several factors: its large checks showed to advantage on wide skirts and bias-cut bodices; it was British in origin; and it referred to the romantic Highlands which were so much appreciated by Queen Victoria. Tartan can be seen in all its woolly glory in Mary Ellen Best's watercolour of her three children, painted in November 1845 (Colour Plate 3). As an Englishwoman living in Germany, the fabric probably reminded her of home. It was not, of course, based on a real clan sett: the fashionable idea of tartan had expanded to include silk fabrics in a variety of non-traditional patterns and colours. These quasi-tartans were worn even by the Princess Royal, Queen Victoria's eldest daughter. Fig. 55 is a silk tartan dress she wore at the age of 10 (*c.* 1850).

The stiffness and tightness of mid nineteenth-century girls' dresses was increased by the habit of lining the bodices with strong calico or glazed cotton with strips of walebone inserted in the seams. Where the bodice was fitted, outer and inner shell were made up together. When the outer layer was cut with drapery, this was mounted on a separate fitted lining (Fig. 56). These linings helped the dress to wear longer and keep cleaner as they could be renewed when it was unpicked for cleaning or remodelling. Most dresses were cleaned infrequently; many silk and wool fabrics were totally unwashable, and even printed cotton could change colour if

Fig. 56   A girl's dress of dull green silk, c. 1850. The ruching on the bodice is held down with narrow ribbon. The skirt flounces are piped to help them stand out. Supposedly worn by a 4-year-old. Length 31 inches (79 cm).

not washed with care. *Cassell's* includes a whole series of recipes for washing different coloured fabrics, using cleaning agents like ammonia or lead acetate depending on the chemical composition of the dyes.[2]

The difficulty of washing was one of the factors which caused resistance to the 'wool next the skin' doctrine; it was not generally accepted until the 1880s, with the advent of mass-produced wool and wool-mix knitted vests and combinations.

It was of course the poorer children engaged in agricultural work or street trades who needed warm clothing most and who were least likely to have access to it. Winter clothing for them might consist of a shawl or an adult's old jacket, possibly a second-hand coat for children living in towns, and perhaps a quilted wool petticoat in the rural areas of Northern England or Wales where these were still worn. Slightly better off children might have home-made petticoats of crocheted wool on a cloth bodice, or frame-knitted 'polka' jackets.

The lack of suitable clothes might in itself form a barrier for girls trying to enter the most common forms of employment such as domestic service and shop work. Shop assistants in the new 'departmental stores' were expected to dress genteelly, often from the stock they sold, regardless of income. Young girls entering service were often told to bring with them all the clothing which they would need for the first year. The only way out was to set

Fig. 57   A pair of drawers, c. 1820–40. They are unusual in having both a central opening and side slits so the back can let down; one would be enough. This type would also be worn by young boys. Length 20 inches (51 cm).

one's sights on a less demanding (and less wealthy) employer, or to apply to one of the charities catering for such cases.[3]

The pattern set for young girls' dresses in the 1840s continued through to the 1860s, with variations in fabric and trimming rather than shape or construction. The long, fitted bodices were set off by long sleeves for day or by short, puffed or 'butterfly' sleeves for evening. Young girls' skirts were worn very short, often only to the knee, with the ends of their broderie anglaise drawers showing beneath. The changes in women's fashion which led to wider and wider skirts supported first by stiffened petticoats and then by wire crinolines, also influenced girls' clothes (Fig. 59). By the 1870s *Cassell's* was recommending a skirt 94 inches (240 cm) wide for an 8-year-old![4] This fullness, combined with extreme shortness, gives a tutu-like effect when seen in fashion plates or photographs. The fullness was produced by starched and frilled petticoats; cage crinolines were worn by older girls whose skirts approached ankle level, but not by younger girls as they would be too revealing when worn under a short skirt.

By the 1860s, more attention was being paid to the cut of girls' clothes, and several types of dress were developed which, while based on adult styles, were felt to be particularly suited to children. Foremost among these was the 'Garibaldi', a pleated

Fig. 58 The Emigrants' Last Sight of Home, *Richard Redgrave, 1858. The girls wear strong cotton print dresses, following fashion only in their sleeves and in the peplum of the youngest girl. Their outdoor clothes consist of 'cottage' bonnets, a sun bonnet, and a frilled cape. All the children including the baby wear pinafores. The boy's is cut with a yoke and almost covers his tunic. They all have strong nailed boots.*

Fig. 59. A girl's alpaca dress trimmed with satin ribbon, late 1860s. Alpaca was a popular fabric which combined the warmth of wool with the sheen of silk. The skirts of this dress would be held out by layers of starched petticoats. Length 41 inches (104 cm).

blouse trimmed with lines of braid, adapted from the peasant costume worn by the Italian patriot and his army. Muslin Garibaldis might be worn with skirts and loose jackets (favoured by Princess Alexandra) in the summer or at the seaside. They might also form the neck and sleeves of what we would call a 'pinafore' dress. These dresses were favoured in the late 1860s when women's fashion was moving into a layered look, with overskirts or tunics worn bunched up over a long underskirt to give a 'bustle' effect.

In the early 1870s there was a new fashion for plain muslin, worn with contrasting silk ribbons. This was partly in reaction to the very brightly coloured silks and velvets which had been worn in the 1860s after the introduction of synthetic dyes. Adult styles which looked far too heavy and overdone on a young girl when executed in silk were refreshingly light and youthful when made up in a muslin, with a light silk underskirt or overdrape.

All of these dresses would have been made either at home or by a small dressmaker, to individual order. In the 1860s there was very little mass-produced clothing, with the exception of semi-fitted items like capes, or clothing for special occasions such as mourning or institutional wear. Sewing machines were coming into use, especially for simpler parts of dresses such as skirt seams and lengths of frilling, but had not yet changed the methods by which garments were made. Some of the first commercial dress-making patterns were published in New York in 1863 by a Mr Butterick, but the cost put these beyond the reach of most home dressmakers. Individually-drawn patterns could also be bought from needlework shops and 'fancy bazaars', but these were even more expensive – as much as 3s. 6d. in the 1850s.[5] For those unwilling or unable to draft their own patterns, the main sources of technical information were paper blocks handed on by friends or needlework teachers, and actual garments. These might be traced over to take the size of the pattern pieces, or unpicked so that the lining could be used to cut out a new garment.

'Patterns' for dressmaking were sometimes advertised in women's magazines; these were actually toiles and were intended mainly for professional dressmakers and priced accordingly. They could be bought either flat or made up, trimmed or plain. The amount of care and work involved in home dressmaking helps to explain the obsession of nineteenth-century educationalists with needlework teaching for girls. It was especially important in the education of working-class girls, both to provide them with a possible employment (though a very badly-paid one), and to instil in them, 'the thrifty disposition, the regularity and neatness, the ideas of order and management' needed by a good housewife and mother.[6]

The reality of these girls' lives was rather different: those, such as Lancashire mill workers, who had money to spend on clothes for themselves and families, often had neither time nor patience for dressmaking. Many others had neither money for new fabric nor energy to make it up. It was for these families that middle-class 'dorcas groups' and church sewing circles provided 'baby boxes' (for loan only), and warm if unglamorous clothing made from mill scraps or recycled flannel petticoats. Instructions on 'How to Make Poor Children's Clothing' were included in needlework books throughout the nineteenth century, and mail-order catalogues were still advertising 'garments for charitable distribution' as late as 1918.[7] No doubt these charitable handouts kept many children warm and healthy, but they could also cause shame when the clothes received were unsuitable in size and style.

Women's fashions of the late 1870s and 1880s were if anything more stifling than those which had gone before. Skirts that had been at least three yards (2.7 m) in circumference since the 1840s had contracted into a narrow tube by 1880. Dresses were usually *en princesse*, and the vertical line was further emphasized by a panel of contrasting colour or texture from waist to hem. These dresses could be either 'natural and comfortable', or 'hideously tight' depending on the taste of the wearer (and the beholder).

Fig. 60 A small girl's Norfolk suit of fine fawn wool, c. 1878, consisting of jacket, blouse and pleated skirt. Suits like this were designed for country wear and anticipated the more tailored styles of the 1890s. Length 26 inches (66 cm).

Fig. 61 A princess dress of blue wool and satin, c. 1880. The straight cut and the ruched and pleated trim reflect women's dresses of the time, though theirs were more tightly fitted. The side drapery shows the beginning of the revived bustle of the 1880s. Length 33 inches (84 cm).

Dress reformers saw them as a vindication of their pleas for lightweight clothing (reduced yardage), loose waists (the princess cut) and sensible underwear (slim-cut combinations replacing the chemise and petticoats). However, any advantages in the new styles for women were soon overcome by the tendency of dressmakers to tighten waists and pile on trimmings. Young girls' short princess dresses came closer to the ideal. These were cut to hang loosely, without the boned darts of women's dresses, although the sleeves fitted tightly. The front panel was often ruched or smocked, techniques favoured by the dress reformers for their rural associations and for the freedom of movement they allowed. Unfortunately in the 1880s smocking was treated purely as a surface decoration and was applied over a fitted lining (Fig. 61 and Colour Plate 6).

By 1885 the female silhouette had slipped backwards into the early 1870s with a revival of the bustle. This time the protuberance was formed not so much by a wire cage as by the dress itself, with swathes of fabric draped over the skirt front and pulled round to the back to fall in bunched pleats. The mass below the waist was offset by tightness above, with long, fitted bodices (sometimes cut smaller than their wearer!) and tight sleeves. This shape was adapted for girls as young as 4, when the knee-length skirts smothered with drapery and bows gave their lower halves a strong resemblance to a solar topi! (Fig. 62).

Fortunately by the mid-1880s there was a much greater variety of sources for those willing to undertake such complicated dressmaking at home. Publications such as *Mrs. Leach's Children's and Young Ladies' Dressmaker* (Fig. 62), founded in 1880, offered a service half-way between that of the mid nineteenth-century women's magazines and later pattern companies. A variety of styles were illustrated in line engraving and described, and readers could send away either for a toile or a paper pattern in several sizes from 6d. upwards. It is interesting to see the different styles and lengths of dresses thought suitable for very small girls (2 to 6

Fig. 62   A group of girls' dresses from Mrs Leach's Children's and Young Ladies' Dressmaker, 1886. The older girls (ages 12 to 16) follow the adult silhouette while the younger girls (ages 4 to 10) are allowed longer and looser waists. The smaller dresses required three to six yards of fabric, the larger ones as much as thirteen yards!

No. **4771**. Walking Dress, 6 to 8 and 8 to 10 Years.   No. **4772**. Morning Costume, 12 to 14 and 14 to 16 Years.   No. **4773**. Washing Dress, 4 to 6 Years.   No. **4774**. The "Brighton" Costume, 12 to 14 and 14 to 16 Years.   No. **4775**. Canvas Costume, 4 to 6 and 6 to 8 Years.

years), young girls (7 to 12 years) and what we would now call teenagers (13 to 16 years). Very small girls' dresses differed from the fashionable norm in having low and less pronounced waists, and bloused bodices. The middle range of outfits kept the low-waisted, short-skirted proportions, but had a more tailored look and were made from women's dress fabrics rather than the machine-made white embroidery which was used for infants' and toddlers' dresses.

The eldest girls' dresses were distinguished from their mothers' only by their slightly shorter length, and by their slightly simpler choice of fabrics and trimmings. Even these simplified styles, however, might be composed of 12 to 15 pattern pieces, using 'eight to ten yards of figured [patterned] and three yards of plain zephyr [lightweight wool] ... six yards of fancy braid' as well as several yards of plain cotton for the lining and the foundation of the bodice. All this for a 'morning costume' for a 12-year-old to wear at home!

By the end of the 1880s there was a radical simplification of girls' clothes, brought about by several factors. One was the establishment of a new type of school dedicated to providing a sound academic education for middle-class girls who were still disbarred from university attendance. These schools, led by the North London Collegiate (founded 1850), stressed physical exercise and intellectual achievement rather than preparation for the 'marriage market'. They had no uniform as such, but encouraged looseness and simplicity of dress:

> I was told after I left that I had been a constant wonder for the length of time one dress had lasted me, and that this had called forth admiration, not contempt. (M. V. Hughes, 1880s)[8]

Some of them required pupils to wear a loose 'gymnasium suit' for all or part of the day.[9]

The movement for higher education for girls was, as yet, confined to a few localities and a handful of 'advanced' families. Most mothers were more influenced by fashion, economy and convenience when dressing their daughters. The last two considerations were catered for by the expanding hosiery industry of the 1880s.

Jackets made of knitted fabric, either plain or openwork, had had a limited vogue since the 1850s, but were generally seen as poor substitutes for tailored garments.[10] However, the brief fashion of 1881 for 'Jersey' outfits, made from cloth of that name and seemingly inspired by the 'Jersey Lily', Lily Langtry, changed the image of knitted fabrics almost overnight. Suddenly they were seen as having the potential to be not merely practical, but, because of their elastic qualities, almost daringly revealing![11] The jersey used for girls' clothes in the 1880s was, however, disappointingly heavy, and usually in neutral colours. It was made up in simple coat-dress shapes similar to Fig. 49 which were easy to care for.[12] Their stretchy fit offered a cheaper alternative to the previous choices of home dressmaking or having garments made to measure.

Knitted dresses were 'not quite the thing' at first, but knitted undergarments were an immediate success. In the early 1880s combinations had been developed for wear under tight fashionable dresses, and their use had spread to children. Made of calico with a multitude of buttons, they were far from comfortable. Knitted combinations of wool or wool-mixtures were a pleasanter alternative, needing fewer fastenings and fitting under the stays with fewer wrinkles.

The final factor that influenced girls' clothes in the late 1880s was the growing degree of borrowing from men's tailoring which was apparent in women's clothes. Sometimes it was a particular garment which was copied, such as the 'Ulster' (a long belted coat) or the 'reefer' jacket worn by sailors. Sports and country clothing took over a number of masculine accessories, including stiff collars, ties and top hats.

A miniature example of this way of thinking can be seen in Fig. 60: it is a small girl's outfit in soft grey tweed, dating from the late 1870s or early 1880s. The skirt is simply pleated all round, and the pleated blouse buttons onto its waistband. Most interesting, however, is the matching jacket worn over the blouse. Its buttoned cuffs, box pleats and belt copy the detailing of a man's Norfolk jacket. Whilst this small ensemble could have been worn in town, the Norfolk detailing, taken from a man's shooting jacket, makes it more likely that it was intended for country wear. A very similar ensemble is shown on an adult in Manet's painting *In the Conservatory*, 1878 (Berlin Museums). The influence of tailoring reached even greater heights in the 1890s, and it will be discussed further in Chapter 8.

In the late eighteenth century and early nineteenth century it seemed as if children's clothes were leading adult dress in the direction of greater freedom and informality. During the middle of the nineteenth century girls' clothes slipped back into their usual role of copying, not initiating, adult fashions. Some concessions were maintained; girls' dresses were generally shorter, looser and slightly simpler than their mothers'. It was not until the 1880s and 1890s that developments in adult clothing – notably the rise of knitted garments and the spread of tailoring for women — combined to give young girls styles which were suited to their needs.

CHAPTER SIX

Boys: 1820-1890

The 1820s were an important decade for boys' clothes, as they marked the end of the skeleton suit which had dominated small boys' wardrobes since the 1780s. With its demise the age of breeching rose as high as eight in the 1860s and 1870s.[1] The widening gap between toddlers' dresses and suits proper was filled by a range of tunics worn with or without trousers.

The skeleton suits of 1820 were different from the originals of 1780, though they kept the distinctive fastening of trousers onto jacket. The trousers were cut to lie flat over the stomach, with no waistband and a wide flap opening (Fig. 63 and Colour Plate 2). Some suits had been made with dark wool jackets and contrasting white cotton trousers since the 1790s, and this was now the dominant fashion.

Slightly older boys had a similar wool jacket which was worn outside and not under the waist of the trousers (Fig. 64). This outfit came closer to contemporary menswear, which had finally accepted trousers for informal use only.[2] The chief differences between the two were the line of the jacket, which was often pointed at back and front, and its lack of coat-tails. The Second Earl Spencer had supposedly originated a tailless jacket of the same name in the 1790s,[3] but this was taken up only by women; men's coats continued with the familiar tails. These small boys' jackets, as well as being tailless, had more extensive trimming than a man's coat; favourite methods were two rows of small covered buttons carried up over the shoulders, and fancy braiding.

Young boys were also distinguished by being allowed to wear open-necked shirts. In the early nineteenth century, gentlemen were excused wearing a necktie only when in a state of undress or when undergoing hard physical labour. This is why the spreading collars of early nineteenth century schoolboys are always shown as beautifully white and crisply laundered: the open shirt was then seen as a sign of youthful freedom and not of distasteful negligence.

From the 1830s onwards, the popularity of the skeleton and 'bellhop' suits was eclipsed, and a different solution was found for

Sister and two brothers, c. 1890. The older boy wears a tailored tweed suit with collar and tie. The younger is at a transitional stage, with long ringlets and a sailor tunic. Underneath can be glimpsed the matching shorts.

Fig. 63 Master Frederick van Diest, John Hoppner. *Although painted in 1810, this is a good example of the skeleton suit of the 1820s, with dark jacket and fitted trousers. A ruff collar was often worn with the high-necked jackets. The low shoes are tied with a ribbon.*

Figure 64 An older boy's suit, 1820–30. The dark green wool jacket is trimmed with braid on cuffs and pockets. The trousers are now straight-cut, with no waistband. They have a double hem to allow for lengthening. This type of suit became the uniform for schoolboys at Eton. Overall length 35 inches (88.5 cm).

Fig. 65 A hussar tunic, c. 1830–35
with a split front and matching
trousers, in pinstriped cotton with
brown wool braid. The trousers are
made like women's drawers. The set
was obviously intended for both
indooor and outdoor wear; it has
detachable long sleeves and a shoulder
cape. It was worn by a boy born in
1828.

clothing young boys who were too old for a dress and too young
for a suit proper. This was the 'tunic suit': a wool jacket with
skirts reaching to the knee, and matching long trousers. These had
been worn since about 1815 and were then made from finely-
striped cotton in a dark colour and trimmed with dark brown or
green wool braid. The tunic was made up with a low bodice and
short sleeves, like a woman's evening dress, but with the skirt front
open from waist to hem. The trousers were sometimes made like a

woman's drawers, with separate legs and shoulder straps. The whole ensemble might be completed by a small cape for outdoor wear and by long sleeves to tie or pin on (Fig. 65).

The decoration of these sets was almost invariably of the hussar type, with lines of braid carried horizontally across the chest and finished with knots or buttons. This represented a particularly appropriate re-borrowing of a motif which had its origins in Hungarian military uniform and enjoyed a brief popularity in masquerade and fancy-dress costumes for men and boys in the late eighteenth century. It was then adopted for women's coats and dresses during the Napoleonic wars, and passed from them back to young boys' dresses and tunics.

Fig. 66 A boy's tunic of 1830–50, in heavy natural cotton. It is similar in outline to a man's greatcoat, but differs in details such as the waist seam and the rows of decorative buttons. It would be worn over trousers like those in Fig. 64 and a shirt like that in Fig. 67. Length 28.5 inches (72 cm).

Plate 5, (left).
Three boys' dresses or tunics, c.1855-70. The red tunic with the cord belt is like those seen in paintings of the 1850s and 1860s. The colour scheme is typical. This tunic was also made in long-sleeved, short-skirted versions to wear over trousers. The orange silk tartan dress is cut on the cross, making the pattern even more striking. It is trimmed with broderie anglaise. The black velvet dress is trimmed with interlaced strips of silk and clusters of steel beads. It is one of a pair worn by two brothers in 1868.

Plate 6, (right).
Two girls' dresses, c.1880-85. The pale blue dress is given interest by a variety of textures — ruching, pleating and fluffy swansdown. The collar and cuffs are of crocheted lace. The light-brown dress has a 'two-piece' effect, with the main part modelled on a late eighteenth-century redingote coat. The smocking on the front panel is still attached to a fitted lining. This outfit was made as a sample for Marshall and Snelgrove, London. The floral embroidery on this dress, and the muted colours of both, are typical of the aesthetic taste of the early 1880s.

Plate 7.
Three girls' dresses, 1937-53. The smallest dress is embroidered with patriotic motifs including flags and a lifebelt for 'HMS Coronation', marking the coronation of George VI in 1937. The patchwork dress was made from scraps of silk and fine cotton for a 5-year-old in 1945. In this example, 'make-do and mend' is transformed from a necessity into a virtue! The smocked dress was made for an 8-year-old in 1953, in a style recalling the 1930s.

Plate 8.
Christening outfit, 1988. The all-in-one suit of stretch fabric, used since the 1960s, is now challenging even that last bastion of tradition, the christening gown. This example is made of acrylic jersey with a quilted satin yoke.

held at the waist with a stout leather belt. Young boys wore this style dress-length over petticoats and white drawers, with a cord rather than a belt at the waist (Colour Plate 5, centre). A similar tunic can be seen in the left corner of Frith's painting *Ramsgate Sands*, 1854. Older boys wore them hip-length over trousers, which now had a fly front. Young boys' tunic dresses could be remodelled as they grew since they were so loosely cut. The main alteration would be to add long sleeves: short sleeves were still a sign of babyhood.

A further option for the transition from skirt to trousers in mid-century was the adoption of quasi-Highland dress. This was popularized by Queen Victoria, whose sons wore kilts when on holiday at Balmoral and even for state occasions such as the opening of the Crystal Palace in 1851.[8] Highland dress was both manly and romantic, and had practical advantages as well. Kilts would not wear out or go out of fashion, and could readily be passed down the family. Furthermore, the bare knees inseparable from this outfit satisfied traditional notions of 'hardening'. However, Highland dress appears not to have caught on in its full form in southern England, being reserved for 'best' occasions if worn at all. Perhaps it was the impractical nature of the velvet jacket with its silver buttons. Perhaps the ensemble was too much like fancy dress. For whatever reason, the cut and fabric of the kilt were frequently borrowed to lend dignity to boys' dresses without invoking the full panoply of Highland costume (see Fig. 105).

During the nineteenth century there seems to have been some uncertainty as to what constituted 'boyish' clothes. For girls it was much simpler; their dresses were always shorter than their mothers', and might have shorter sleeves and looser waists, but

Fig. 69   A Dame's School, Thomas Webster, 1845. Most of the boys are dressed like their fathers in short jackets, strong wool or corduroy trousers (turned up to keep them clean) and stout boots. Several wear smocks. One boy is better dressed, with a tailored coat. The hats by the door are either flat caps or soft felt.

Fig. 70 *Phillip Wilson Todd, photographed by Lewis Carroll, c. 1865. He wears the classic boy's suit of the 1860s, with an open jacket, waistcoat and knickerbockers The edges bound with braid are a typical detail.*

otherwise followed their elders' in outline and construction. During the late eighteenth century, boys clothing had been longer in the leg and tighter in the body than their fathers'. By the 1830s menswear had caught up, and the silhouette of both younger and older boys was reasonably like that of a man; the older boy's jacket was like a man's dress coat minus its tails, and the younger boy's tunic followed the lines of a man's greatcoat.

In the early 1860s a new experiment was tried, that of making boys' clothing both shorter and wider than the adult prototype.

Male and female clothing was becoming more voluminous, with the introduction of wide 'paletot' jackets for men and skirts supported by wire cages for women. This new aesthetic led to the introduction of knickerbockers for boys. They were worn full, like plus-fours, and fastened below the knee; this helped to hold up the long wool stockings worn by boys as well as girls. With them was worn a matching waistcoat, now with front points, and a curious jacket with cutaway fronts which fastened only at the neck so that the whole of the waistcoat front was exposed (Fig. 70).

The most popular fabric for this ensemble was a neutral-coloured wool tweed, with the seams trimmed with contrasting braid. These suits frequently appear in photographs and were evidently favoured for everyday wear. They could be varied by making the trousers straight and open-ended like long shorts for a young boy, or by cutting them as trousers proper for an older boy. Although so many pictures of this outfit are known, very few examples survive, perhaps because they were so much worn. One suit in Bath Museum of Costume has the long trousers proper for an older boy but still retains the open jacket.

The open jacket and the vaguely 'Turkish' nature of the trousers gave these suits their contemporary name of 'zouave' ensembles. The zouaves were an Algerian volunteer regiment who fought on the side of the French in the Crimean War of 1854–6. They were known for their picturesque costumes which included what we would call 'bolero' jackets.[9] Long after their origins were forgotten, open fronted jackets were still considered as particularly suitable for boys – again a reminder of 'hardening', perhaps.

Knickerbocker suits were worn only by older boys in the 1860s and 1870s; Cassell's assumes that boys of 6 and 7 would wear tunics! A transitional outfit for this age group was a tunic or jacket and skirt worn over matching knickerbockers or short trousers.[10] The late age of breeching may be related to the beginning of formal schooling. When Cassell's describe knickerbockers, they also give instructions for marking a boy's clothing for boarding school. Eight-year-old boys from working families would be nearing the end of their formal education, which might have begun at 3 or 4. When compulsory school attendance was introduced in 1876, the school-leaving age was only 10.[11] Mid nineteenth-century paintings of village schools show the youngest boys still wearing dresses.[12] Poorer families were less able to indulge in subtle gradations of dress according to age and sex than were the status-conscious middle classes.

If Highland dress and the zouave jacket had a slight element of fancy dress in them, the garments which became the most popular choice for late nineteenth-century boys in England and elsewhere were a faithful copy of an exotic uniform. This was, of course, the sailor suit. This style was based on the standardized naval uniform that was introduced in the 1840s along with regularized pay and recruitment.

It was in this new uniform (summer version) that the painter

Winterhalter was asked to depict the young Prince of Wales (later Edward VII) in 1846 (Colour Plate 4). His outfit of white cotton drill faced with blue and trimmed with white braid is complete down to the details of the black silk neckerchief and the small knife hung from a cord belt (for splicing or cutting ropes).[13] It had in fact been ordered from the official naval outfitters.

This early enthusiasm for sailor suits correct in every detail took some time to spread outwards from the Royal family. Sailor suits were not generally popular until the 1870s, by which time the Prince of Wales had two sailor-suited sons of his own. Manufacturers capitalized on Royal tastes by advertising sailor suits 'as worn by the Royal princes'.[14] These suits were not as close to naval uniform as Edward VII's had been. In Fig. 71, the main nautical features are the blue cotton facings trimmed with white braid, which contrast with the natural linen of the body of the suit. The long, buttoned-back lapels are borrowed from military rather than naval uniform, there is no 'sailor collar', and the trousers are the open-ended shorts popular for young boys in the 1870s. They do not even have the front flap opening (carried down from the eighteenth century) which characterized true naval bell-bottoms.

Fig. 71   A sailor suit, c. 1876, in natural linen with blue facings and white braid. The jacket is more military than naval in shape. Long shorts replaced knickerbockers in the 1870s. The spade is original. Length 28 inches (71 cm).

These 'nautical' suits reflected the growing popularity of seaside holidays among the middle classes, encouraged by the establishment of an efficient railway network. For prolonged seaside visits it was necessary to have clothes which would stand up well to sun and salt water; women's seaside dresses were often of white cotton piqué trimmed with interlaced patterns in narrow green or black braid. As seaside towns were fashionable resorts in the 1860s and 1870s, what was worn there influenced the rest of fashionable life as *après ski* fashions did in the 1970s and 1980s.

It is easy to understand that the semi-fantasies of 'sailor' or 'Highland' clothes were not relevant to the young working-class boys who formed the majority of the age-group. Up to 1876 there were few restrictions on child employment, except in the textile industry where boys and girls aged 9 to 13 worked a 'humane' eight-hour day. The school-leaving age, established at 10 years in 1876, was only raised gradually, and stood at 12 in 1900. Even then, children could leave earlier in cases of special need, and were often proud to do so: 'I wanted to tell the world I was now a man, working and helping my mother.' (Jack Lanigan, aged 10, 1900)[15]

In some areas such as the cotton towns of Lancashire there was provision for children working in the mills to attend school half-time, and this could involve two completely different sets of clothes: 'We half-timers knocked-off at half-past twelve; then it was a race home for a quick meal, change from corduroys and scarf into knicker-bockers and collar and button-on bow, then a final dash to Spotland school at two o'clock.' (James Brady, aged 11, 1909)[16] On going full-time, the childish knickerbockers would be left off in favour of a working man's corduroy trousers, neckerchief and cloth cap.

In these circumstances, childhood was seen as a brief period in

which it might be possible to learn something useful before commencing paid work, and children's clothing was largely defined by the financial standing of the family. The 'respectable' working classes, the families of artisans and labourers in steady employment, were often defined by their ability to clothe their children decently, with strong boots or shoes, and perhaps a change of clothes for Sunday. One step lower down were the indigent working classes, employed in low-paid jobs such as sweated tailoring, or suffering from unemployment. In these families it was a struggle to clothe children at all: boots, and even underwear, might be sacrificed at the pawnshop in order to pay the rent. It was for children such as these that 'ragged schools' were set up as places where they might get some instruction without any fear of criticism on account of their appearance.

Even before they were fully part of the working world, poorer children's clothes reflected their parents' callings. Country boys might wear a smock or short double-breasted jacket over corduroy or moleskin trousers cut short to be worn with leather gaiters and stout boots (Fig. 69). Young cockneys reflected their parents' pride in their calling by sporting miniature costermonger's suits. A coster boy is placed in the centre foreground of Frith's painting *Derby Day*, 1856, and can be recognized by his velveteen jacket and the loop of rope to help steady a heavy basket on his head. Boys from fishing families often wore knitted 'ganseys' and heavy serge trousers – one of Frank Meadow Sutcliffe's Whitby photographs shows a small boy, still 'in petticoats', but with his own miniature gansey and sou'wester.[17] The great levelling of sartorial differences was to come only in the 1890s, with the application of mass-production methods to tailoring.

Fig. 72 A Fauntleroy Suit in purple plush, worn by a 7-year-old to watch Queen Victoria's Jubilee procession in 1887. The collar and cuffs are of Irish crochet lace. This outfit, influenced by seventeenth-century dress, was popularized by Frances Hodgson Burnett's novel Little Lord Fauntleroy, *1886. Length 33.5 inches (85 cm).*

CHAPTER SEVEN

Babies: 1890-1985

Between 1820 and 1890, infant's clothes had undergone many superficial changes in materials, cut, and decoration, but there had been surprisingly few real changes. Up to the ages of crawling and toddling, they were still dressed in a vest or shirt, a linen, wool, or quilted band to support the stomach, several petticoats, and a low-necked, sleeveless dress with a skirt up to a yard long. A long cloak with four or more yards of fabric hanging from the ribbon tie at the neck, and a hat or hood of silk stiffened with quilting or cord, were added for outdoor wear. There had been some advances in the treatment of the very young; the monthly gown, with high neck and long sleeves had become accepted wear for the newborn.

With the introduction of new absorbent fabrics such as 'Turkish' or 'terry' towelling, a debate had opened as to the proper material for babies' nappies, which were formerly made from linen 'diaper' weave. Further debate centred on the healthiness or otherwise of the new mackintosh 'pilches' worn over the nappy. These were said to 'make the wet napkin into a most unhealthy fomentation'.[1]

In 1890, these new developments were still filtering their way through society. They were aided by the emphasis given to homecraft and infant care in the education of the mothers of the future sons of empire. The Harrods catalogue issued in 1895 illustrates many garments which were in use a decade before, including a long gown with a princess front made up of many strips of machine-made embroidery (Fig. 46). It also shows a new type called the 'New American Shape' which differs in several respects from those previously in use. It is like the monthly gown in having a high neck, long sleeves, and no front panel; yet it differs from them in having not a bodice but a yoke ending at the armholes. This 'new' gown is also elaborately trimmed around the hem, with groups of pintucks alternating with lace insertions and machine-embroidered flounces. Each element of the trimming is rather insignificant, but grouped together in a band up to 12 inches (30 cm) deep they make a good effect. The small yokes are often

A boy aged 1 in 1902. The smock-shaped 'shortening' dress would still reach his shoes. The hem trimming, with several rows of insertion, is typical.

[103]

entirely made up of strips of lace insertion from a half to one inch (1.3–2.5 cm) wide, hemstitched together.

The position of the trimming on these new-style dresses, and its delicacy, derived from trends in adult female fashion. Women's dresses in the mid-1890s had a great deal of shoulder interest, expressed through huge 'leg of mutton' sleeves, epaulettes and beaded yokes. Looser, flowing styles carried out in lightweight silks had come into favour in reaction to the heavily upholstered fashions of the late 1880s. Skirts were wider, with rows of trimming above the flared hems. There was even a limited acceptance of the 'smock' style advocated by the dress reformers, though this was restricted to informal garments such as teagowns. All of these influences can be seen in the new baby gowns, with their full sleeves, shoulder trim, and hem decoration. The new fullness of cut was also seen in older girls' dresses (see Chapter 8), carried out in heavier fabrics.

There were some things which had not changed, notably the way in which these dresses were manufactured. Although both the embroidered trimmings and the lace for insertions were now generally machine-made, machine sewing was looked down on when it came to making-up. This may partly have been a result of the plethora of fine tucks and insertions which would have shown up any carelessness in machine stitching. Yet the advertisements for high-class dresses emphasize that they are completely hand made – including the side seams. The resistance to machine sewing derived partly from a feeling that only hand-stitching was 'good enough' for the precious infant: 'surely nothing can come up to the home-made, well-thought-out, love-stitched little wardrobe'.[2]

The introductions to sewing books published as late as the 1930s could still state that 'baby clothes in which every possible operation is done by machine are inclined to look a little stereo-typed and cheap'.[3] This snobbery about hand sewing resulted in the extension of 'sweating' into the early twentieth century to satisfy the demand for hand-made babywear and lingerie items (Fig. 73). The attitude to machine sewing had been different in the mid nineteenth century; when domestic machines were first introduced they were designed as parlour ornaments and featured as accessories in fashion plates.[4]

The accessories worn with the new 'round' dresses relied on subtle trimming and beautiful textures rather than on visual contrasts for their effect, unlike the bold two-tone capes of the 1870s. White or cream had become the invariable colours for babies' cloaks and hoods, which were executed in wool flannel, serge or cashmere for winter, and cambric or piqué for summer. Ruffles of machine-embroidered silk on the edge of the cloak and cape and around the hood were a favourite trimming in the mid-1890s. An alternative was silk floss embroidery of twined floral sprays round the cape and hem. This could be worked at home using patterns traced from a women's magazine or from the newly available iron-on embroidery transfers.

Fig. 73   A very elaborate babygown of c. 1910. The curved stripe of insertion is also found on women's petticoats of this date. The machine-lace insertions and flounces are joined by decorative hemstitching. Length 40 inches (102 cm).

One of the most interesting aspects of the late nineteenth-century and early twentieth-century clothing industry is the appearance of not one, but several markets for mass-produced garments. Earlier in the century, such garments as were available ready-made were aimed clearly at particular social groups; early nineteenth-century Ayrshire-work gowns were priced too high for any but the wealthy. Poorer families had to make their own clothes, buy second hand, or rely on charity. This changed with the introduction of machine-based methods of making up and trimming, and it was then possible for poorer families to obtain a cheap facsimile of fashionable styles.

This change can be seen quite clearly in the mail-order catalogues which began to appear in the late 1890s. Some of these were sale catalogues for established businesses, such as Harrods, while others represented a mail-order only firm. The price and quality of the goods on offer varied widely, with several qualities available within one catalogue. The Army and Navy Stores, London, had as the top of their 1907 range of baby gowns a 'handsome embroidered muslin robe' for £2.15s. (Fig. 73). The average working-class wage at this time was £1.6s. a week.[5] Cheaper gowns cost between 4s. 11d. and 16s. 6d., depending on the amount of lace and embroidery and whether it was worked by hand or machine.

Compare this with a price-list from The Bradford Manufactur-

Fig. 74 Two children's bibs c. 1890–20. Both are made of linen, with inscriptions woven in red. 'Don't talk too loud' may be a catchphrase from a contemporaneous popular song.

ing Co. for 1910. This was clearly aimed at less wealthy families although the styles shown are in line with contemporary fashions. Their 'Christening Robes' range in price from 5s. 11d. to 14s. 11d. for the 'superior quality'; with a 'very handsome Jap Silk Robe' forming the summit at £1. 1s. 6d. Their monthly gowns, with less trimming, are cheaper still at 2s. 6d. to 4s. 11d. compared with 4s. 6d. to 14s. 9d. at the Army and Navy Stores.

There is some evidence that children's items were being produced specifically to meet the tastes of the prosperous working classes. Small items such as bibs were woven or printed with humorous expressions like 'Our Pet' and 'Don't talk too Loud' (Fig. 74). These were the beginning of a long tradition of using slogans or images from popular culture, to be followed in the 1920s with embroidery transfers based on characters from comics, and in the 1950s with Disney characters.

By the 1920s the situation had changed decisively, and the vast majority of manufactured goods were aimed at the middle class and prosperous working class. Hand-made gowns with masses of tiny insertions were now the exception, restricted to those who could either afford to buy them from exclusive shops or who had both time and skill to make them at home.

Sewing machines were becoming increasingly popular, though still relatively expensive, and there was a boom in home dressmaking encouraged by the greater availability and reliability of paper patterns. Sewing manuals aimed at mothers discouraged them from using their machines to emulate shopbought finery, and instead urged them to make garments that were serviceable and would wear and wash well. The last consideration was especially important, as there was a steady drop in the availability of servants to help with chores such as washing after the First World War.

For those who wanted to save money but were less able seamstresses it was also possible to buy partly made-up garments in which the side seams were sewn to fit the child. These were sold by Harrods in 1917 for 14s. 9d. For 1s. or 1s. 6d. a mother could buy a yoke and sleeves to be transformed into a robe with the addition of a few yards of machine-embroidered fabric (Bradford Manufacturing Co., 1910).

Although the cut and making-up of babies' garments were simpler in the 1920s than they had been in 1890, the number of items needed stayed the same. Flannel petticoats were still considered necessary, as were stiff linen binders. Carrying cloaks were going out of fashion, superseded by knitted shawls for the very young, and matinée jackets or caped pelisse-coats for older babies. One major simplification of the wardrobe had been achieved: the blurring of the distinction between the 'long clothes' worn for the first few months of life and the second or 'shortening' set. 'We follow now the plan of making the layette neither very long nor very short, and roomy enough to last the child most of the first year.'[6] Another was the choice of raglan rather than set-in sleeves for dresses and nightgowns (Fig. 79).

B. B. EVANS & CO. High Road, KILBURN, N.W. 6.

Sale of Everything for
CHILDREN

These can all be Bought
by Post.

U 452—INFANTS WHITE
WOOL COATS, with
Pink or Blue collars
and cuffs, 14 in.

17/11

U 452

Layettes machine made
up to **£3/3/0**

Also hand made from **£3/3/0**
to **£8/8/0**
Details on application.

U 457—CHILD'S TEAZEL
WOOL COAT,
size 14, 16, 18;
32/-, 34/, 36/-
Caps to match
7/6

U 457

Set 1—Infant's Complete Layette,
comprising 2 Night Gowns, 2 Day Gowns,
2 Long Flannels, 1 Wool Head Shawl,
2 Vests, 2 Cotton Swathes, 6 Turkish Squares, 1 Puff, 1 Powder
Box, 1 Packet of Powder,
Bundle of Nursery Pins,
as illustrated.

34/11

U 453—CHILD'S SMOCKED
OVERALL, White ground,
with Pink, Blue or Red
shots, 18 in. **3/11¾**

POST ORDERS
receive prompt and
careful attention.

U 451—INFANTS' WOOL
HAND-MADE COATS.
White only ... **9/11**

U 458—INFANTS' WHITE
WOOL BOOTS. **1/11½**

U 450—INFANTS' LARGE
WHITE WOOL SHAWLS,
as illustrated. **16/11**
We hold a large stock of
SHAWLS, from 6/11 to
£5.5.0

U 455—CHILD'S WHITE
COTTON MATTE CLOTH
OVERALL, hand embroid-
ered, with coloured silk
fancy borders, as sketched
or with animals.
Overalls, 19 in. ... **7/11**
Knickers to match, **3/11½**

Shop by Post.

Fig. 75 *A page from the catalogue of
B. B. Evans, Kilburn, c. 1920. The
'Complete Layette, 34s. 11d.' includes
only two of each main garment, and
six nappies.*

Manufacturers and parents of the mid nineteenth century had
expended most of their money and attention on the newborn
infant, who was provided with lavishly embroidered dresses and
delicate caps. In the early twentieth century attention shifted to the
crawler and toddler, and it is in these age groups that innovations
are to be found.

Earlier toddlers had been dressed in shortened versions of the
baby's gown, dresses which were literally made-over from baby
dresses, or alluded to them in their use of white, embroidered
fabrics. Children who were learning to walk would be given
drawers over their nappies, but this was as much to spare the sensi-
bilities of their families as to help them. Sometimes the drawers
were made large enough to button on over the petticoats to keep
them clean. A 'crawling overall' had been recommended by
Cassell's: 'The best dress for the crawlings age is one in which little
French children are usually attired – a sort of knickerbocker suit,
warm and loose, with trousers and vest all in one piece.'[7]

However, these were not generally known in Britain until about
1918, when they start to appear in mail-order catalogues. Harrods
offered 'rompers' for the first time in 1919, at prices from 6s. 11d.
These were made like a small boiler suit, with long sleeves, a
yoked bodice, short knickerbocker legs, and a drop seat concealed
by the waist belt. In plain fabrics which could be easily laundered,
and with less bulk around the knees and body than traditional petticoats, they were a convenience for both mother and child. They
were quickly taken up by a number of major retailers and Harrods
also offered versions to fit boys up to 5 years old (Fig. 108).

The popularity of romper suits and crawling overalls may have
been owed to American influences on both mass-produced and
home-made clothing. Romper suits had been sold by the American

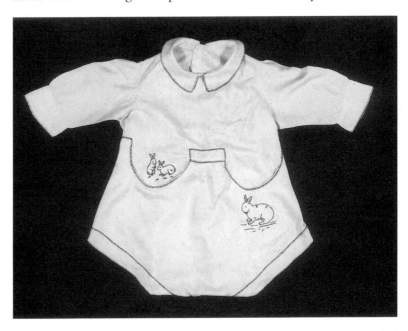

Fig. 76 *An early boys' romper suit,
c. 1915–20, in natural silk with red
embroidery. It gives the impression of
a shorts set, though made in one piece.
It fastens at the crotch with buttons.*

Fig. 77   *A small boy's smock in green Viyella, c. 1935. An almost identical garment is illustrated as 'Sonny's first suit' in a Weldon's 'Tiny Tots' pattern book.*

mail-order firm Sears Roebuck since 1910,[8] and they also feature in a set of dressmaking booklets published in 1922 by the *Women's Institute of Domestic Science*, Pennsylvania.[9] These booklets illustrate several practical styles including rompers made to look like shorts and a shirt for young boys, and dresses with matching bloomers for young girls.

During the 1920s there was a tendency to differentiate between boys' and girls' clothing at an increasingly early age. One way of doing this was through colour, although the modern convention of 'pink for a little girl, blue for a boy' was not fully established until the 1930s. As late as 1921, the *Women's Institute* booklets were recommending the opposite choice of colours. Young boys' clothes were more simply made and trimmed than their sisters', but still showed a great deal of variety in colour and fabric (Fig. 77).

Another factor which changed babies' and young children's clothing in the 1920s was the increasing use of knitted dresses, jerseys, kilts, coats and hats. This movement was accelerated by the relaxation of manners during the First World War, when knitted 'sports coats' became all the rage for women. This period also saw the introduction of novelty yarns which increased the attractions of home knitting; first angora and 'teasel wool', used to make warm coats and hats, and then rayon.

Rayon was the first synthetic fibre and it filled the demand for a material which would look and hang like silk, but be cheaper and more durable. It was very quickly taken up for women's hosiery (which it dominated until the advent of nylon), for satin lingerie and for home knitting. Early rayon yarn was not particularly suited to children's wear, being cold to the touch and very heavy, but its silky look outweighed its disadvantages. Countless knitting patterns were published throughout the 1920s and 1930s for sets of dress and knickers or tunic and knickers, simply shaped and trimmed with a band of angora (Fig. 78). Girls' versions had more trimming and a wider skirt, while boys' were left plain.

By the 1920s, the perambulator or baby-carriage had been fully accepted in all levels of society that could afford it.[10] Current thinking on childcare said that babies should have an 'airing' for several hours every day, even to the extent of having a cot placed in the back garden. As the covers and blankets of the pram hid the child's lower half, clothes for outdoor wear concentrated on decorating the chest and head. This was a complete contrast to the late nineteenth-century baby, whose status was proclaimed by the long folds of shawl or 'carrying mantle' draped over the nurse's arm.

These outing sets consisted of a short coat or matinée jacket and matching hat. Knitted 'overalls' could be worn to fill the chilly gap under short skirts. These were what we would now call tights; the name was perhaps taken from the military term overalls, meaning tight trousers. For older children who had started to walk, these might have 'gaiter' feet, with false buttons at the ankles and straps to hold them under the foot. Above the age of 2 or 3, the same function would be fulfilled by shaped cloth gaiters with buttons

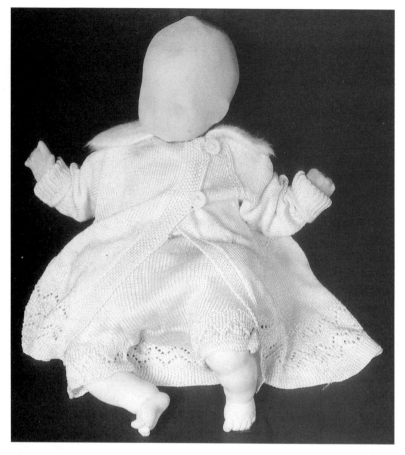

Fig. 78 A 'pram set' of coat and knickers hand-knitted in cream rayon yarn, c. 1920. The angora collar is a typical touch. Coat length 14.5 inches (37 cm).

from ankle to thigh. These were worn both by girls and by boys who were still in tunics and short trousers, and can be seen in the illustrations to A. A. Milne's books of poems.

The war years and after

The declaration of war in 1939 did not immediately alter the market for babies' and children's clothes. For many of the infants born during the period of the 'phoney' war, life was more prosperous than it had been for their elder brothers and sisters, as unemployed fathers were called up for the army and essential industries.

As the war progressed, bombing raids, evacuation and semi-compulsory war-work disrupted the patterns of family life. In 1941 a system of rationing for clothes and basic foods was introduced; special food allowances were made available to babies and pregnant women, though these still had to be paid for. Government departments responsible for public health and welfare published morale-boosting leaflets advising mothers how to feed and clothe their families.

Wartime mothers were subjected to a variety of contradictory pressures: from industry to take up war-work, from their families to provide missing comforts, and from the government to save for war-bonds and to economize by 'make-do and mending' their own and their children's clothes. Skill in 'make-do and mend' swiftly became a necessity in order to eke out the garments available on the ration points. Adults and children were each allocated 66 clothing coupons to last a year, and babies were allowed 40. The coupon values of items of clothing, knitting wool and cloth were specified – a baby's short dress or petticoat took two coupons, while a pram set or long dress needed three. Even nappies were rationed, at a coupon each, later reduced to half a coupon (Fig. 83).[11]

Further restrictions were imposed by the 'Utility' scheme, introduced in 1942 to cover clothing and household goods. The amount of fabric and trimming in manufactured garments was strictly limited; a baby's rayon satin dress might have pintucks or em-

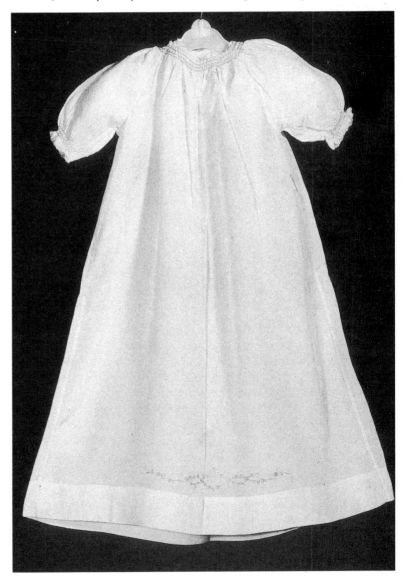

Fig. 79   A raglan-sleeved babygown in silk crêpe, 1939. The simple shape would be equally suited to a nightgown, but the coloured smocking and embroidery make it suitable for day wear. Home-made. Length 26 inches (67 cm).

Fig. 80 A Utility babygown in rayon satin, c. 1946. Utility features are the lack of lace or embroidery, and the shortness of the skirt. A gown like this would have required 3 coupons, and cost about 15 s. Length 24 inches (61 cm).

broidery, but not both, and was not to exceed 24 inches (61 cm) in length (Fig. 80).

As the war continued, many women grew tired of these restrictions and unofficial solutions to the clothing problem were sought. One of the favourites was to make up underwear and baby clothes from parachute panels. These were made of strong silk, almost like nylon; each panel, made of joined lengths, contained enough fabric for a small child's dress. Women who were fortunate enough to have one of these would often be asked to lend the finished garment to the less fortunate (Fig. 82).

By 1945 most British families hoped for a return to peace-time prosperity, but this took a while to come. Rationing of clothes continued until 1949 and of food until 1954. The influence of the war years was seen in several types of garments which remained popular into the 1950s. One of these was a hooded sleeping-bag for babies, first introduced in the 1930s.[12] This gained popularity during the war as a 'shelter bag' to keep babies warm during night-time air-raids.

A garment which fulfilled the same purpose for older children was the 'siren suit', made like a boilersuit of thick wool cloth with a front zip (Fig. 96). During the war these were made in both child and adult sizes (and were worn, famously, by Winston Churchill). Unfortunately both shelter bags and siren suits were taken off the manufacturers' lists of permitted garments in 1944 by an over-zealous revision of the Utility regulations. Siren suits crept back after the war in the guise of the 'snow suit', opening down the body and inside leg. These were offered by Grattan in 1951 for £3. 18s. to £4. 15s. 11d.

There was a great interest in new styles and new materials in the late 1940s and early 1950s. By far the most important of these was the 'wonder fibre', nylon. It had been patented by Du Pont in 1938 but was not available to British civilians until 1946. News of it had filtered out during the war, and by the time it reached the public there was a massive demand. It was used initially for ladies' hosiery, but was also popular for sheer fabrics. Its 'easy care' properties made it a natural choice for toddlers clothes, where it was overprinted with flock to give a lace effect, or woven into

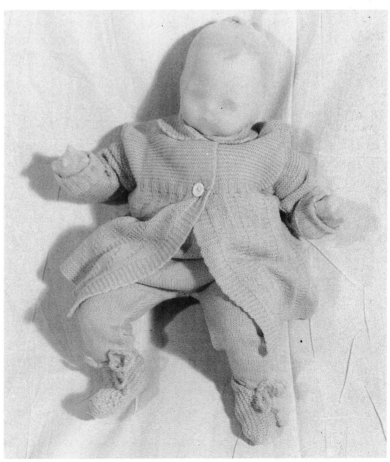

Fig. 81   A Utility pramset, machine-knitted in pale-blue wool, c. 1945–9. This outfit shows fewer signs of Utility restrictions. A similar set cost 19 s. and 3 coupons in 1949.

bubbly seersucker. Its greater tensile strength made it more adaptable than rayon, and by the 1960s nylon was being made into lace fabric and trimmings and even patterned tights for toddlers (Fig. 85).

The romper suit had now been accepted as the standard garment for babies over 6 months old and for toddlers. Paradoxically this led to more, not fewer, differences between very young boys' and girls' clothes. Boys no longer wore smocks and tunics, and their romper suits were often made to give the impression of shorts and shirt (Fig. 84). This had been done in the 1930s, but not for boys under 2 years old!

In the late 1960s babies' and toddlers' dresses followed the trends in women's fashions and became shorter and A-line in cut. They were often made so short that frilled nylon pants became a visible part of the outfit! Nylon and other synthetics such as Terylene continued to be much in fashion, though they needed more careful washing than the traditional cotton. Underclothing had been simplified down to a vest and one or more petticoats, with only the vest still made of wool. The binder or belt had finally disappeared.

One of the most important items in the modern baby's wardrobe was invented in the late 1950s, though it was not widely used until the 1960s.[13] This was the 'babygrow', an all-in-one garment combining elements of the romper suit and of the pram set, and made of fleecy knitted fabric. When first introduced it was made without decoration and was regarded as nightwear. In 1969, the first year it appeared in Grattan's catalogue, a plain white

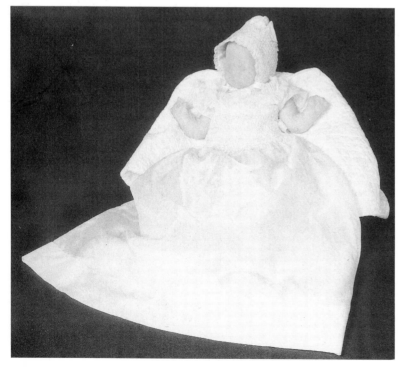

Fig. 82 (left)   An example of 'make-do-and-mend', 1944; a christening gown, cap and cape made from a panel of parachute silk. The dress and cap are smocked, the cape is machine-quilted. Made by a woman living in an area of Bristol badly affected by bombing, and loaned out to friends' babies.

Fig. 83 (right)   A page from a Grattan mail order catalogue of 1949, the year rationing ended. Some of the garments, like the flannel 'Barra' petticoat and the 'binder' belt, have hardly changed since the 1840s. Both of these were eventually discontinued in the 1950s.

DAINTY FOR BABY

C 542 · · · · · · · · · ·
Our Agents must allow Customers a Discount of 9d. in the £ on all Cash purchases

C 293. All-Wool Cosy BARRAS, made from a good quality flannel, neatly bound edges. **PRICE 4/2**
2 Coupons

C 291. Infants' NIGHTDRESS in good quality Cream Winceyette.
3 Coupons **PRICE 5/2**

C 792. Babies' Cosy All-Wool FLANNEL BINDERS, bound at edges and nicely made, approximately 5 ins. in width. **PRICE 2/-**
4 Binders for 1 Coupon

C 561. A superior quality All-Wool Wincey NIGHTGOWN finished tie neck, wrists and all-round tie belt. Colour: Cream **PRICE 7/7**
3 Coupons

C 295. Baby's WRAPPER VEST in All-Wool. Made with a good wrap-over and ties with ribbon. **PRICE 4/2**
2 for 1 Coupon

R 306. White Turkish Nursery NAPKINS in useful size: 22 × 22 ins. **PRICE 23/2**
6 Coupons per Dozen

S 732
A charming CHRISTENING ROBE in superior quality Art Crepe. Full gathered skirt on to a daintily embroidered yoke. Puff sleeves and neat frill at the neck. A lovely garment for a happy event. Colour: Ivory
PRICE 16/3
3 Coupons

C 542
Infants' PETTICOAT in Art. Silk Locknit. Neatly made and finished. Length 16 ins. Colour: Ivory
PRICE 2/11
2 Coupons

C 289
Infants' PETTICOAT in nice quality Cream Winceyette. Length 16 inches. **PRICE 2/10**
2 Coupons

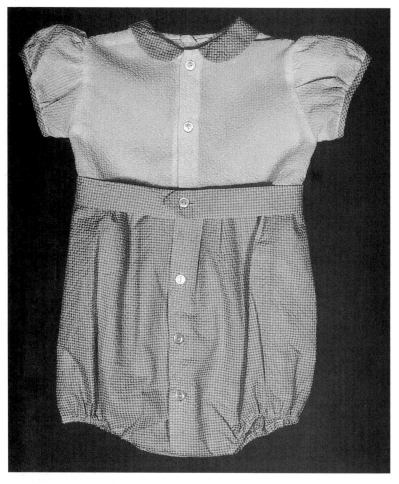

Fig.. 84 A small boy's romper set of nylon seersucker, c. 1950–2. The bottom half is made of a darker fabric to look like shorts. It opens down the front and between the legs. Length 18.5 inches (47 cm).

version cost 17s. 11d. as compared to £1. 5s. or more for a dress. It has gradually gained acceptance for round-the-clock wear, and is now available in brightly coloured stripes and prints from all the major manufacturers. Recently these suits, suitably trimmed in white satin and lace, have even challenged that last bastion of tradition, the christening gown (Colour Plate 8).

Even more significant for most mothers has been the increased availability of the disposable nappy. These have been on the market since the 1890s; Harrods advertised 'sanitary wood wool napkins' at 1s. 4d. to 1s. 10d. per dozen in 1895. These were supposed to 'dispense with the constant changing of ordinary napkins, prevent all irritation, soreness and liability to chill'. They were not immediately popular because of the cost of repeated purchases (re-usable nappies cost from 5s. 6d. to 10s. 6d. per dozen in the same catalogue) and because of the difficulties of supply.

Other attempts were made to redesign the nappy from 1910 onwards, one of the more successful being 'Harrington's Squares'. These were made of several thicknesses of muslin and could be used on their own for newborns or as a liner for older children. Another variant was the 'Stork' nappy which offered to 'save

Fig. 85   *A christening gown of nylon lace fabric, 1972. The fullness, hem decoration, robings and use of lace look back to the traditional christening gown although the fabrics and techniques used are typical of the late twentieth century.*

work, [and] prevent bow legs'. It was a triangle of plain cloth, with a panel of towelling the shape of a bicycle seat.[14] During the Second World War soap was rationed, and mothers were recommended to save on nappy-washing by using cotton wool pads or even bags of sphagnum moss.[15] In spite of all these false starts, disposable nappies as we know them did not become generally available until the 1960s.

In recent years sportswear has been a major influence on adults' and children's clothes, and has even spread downwards to babies until we have 'tracksuits' and 'jogging suits' for infants barely able to crawl! Both boy and girl toddlers' clothing is increasingly modelled on adult leisurewear made from stretchy knitted fabrics, and tailored dresses and suits are worn only for 'best'. It seems as if the knitwear industry has finally achieved the simplification of infants' clothing which has been the goal of reformers since the 1740s.

CHAPTER EIGHT

Girls: 1890-1985

The 1890s were a decade in which two contradictory trends in women's fashion became increasingly prominent. The first was the adoption of shapes and fabrics taken from menswear, at first for active sports and then for everyday clothes. These 'tailor-made' outfits had a plain skirt and fitted jacket of dark wool cloth, worn with a white shirt or blouse and even with a collar and tie. Suits like this, simplified to a white blouse and dark skirt for indoor wear, provided a much-needed 'working dress' for the growing numbers of women working in professions such as teaching and the Civil Service. There was another side to contemporary fashion which became increasingly important towards the end of the 1890s. Its characteristics were wide gored skirts with trimmed and flounced hems, blouses of soft draping fabrics, and a multitude of delicate trimmings

Clothing for girls was caught between these two extremes, the mannish 'New Woman' on the one hand, and the creature of the boudoir on the other. The way in which mothers chose to dress their daughters reflected their aspirations for them. Girls who attended schools which aimed to develop their physical and intellectual capacity were likely to wear plain, tailored styles, even when the school had no uniform as such. For those receiving a traditional education at home, or for holiday times, more elaborate materials and styles would be allowed.

Sailor suits were as popular for young girls' school and holiday wear as they were for their brothers'. The associations of sailor suits with little boys helped to detract from any excessively masculine connotations. The blouse of the suits might be an exact copy of the navy blue serge 'midshipman's blouse' worn by a brother (perhaps even a hand-me-down); or it might be made of white cotton or linen with a blue sailor's collar. The former type was usually bought ready-made from firms such as John Noble of Manchester ('GUARANTEED MADE WITHOUT SWEATING') who specialized in women's 'ready-to-wear'. Boys' outfitters such as Barran's of Leeds also found girls' sailor suits a worthwhile sideline (Fig. 87). The white blouses could be made up at home or

Four sisters, c. 1910. The eldest, aged 16, has calf-length skirts and long sleeves. The younger girls aged 4–9 show progressively more leg and arm the younger they are. Although it is summer, they all wear black stockings and strong boots.

Fig. 86 Children's clothes c. 1900–10. The elder girl wears a smock-dress of blue linen, the younger girl a skirt and blouse of blue cotton with 'Swiss' embroidery. The boy wears a summer sailor suit of white cotton.

by a 'little dressmaker'. Sailor suits were occasionally worn as late as the 1920s.[1]

Apart from the blouse and skirt, the most important innovation for girls during the 1890s, was the yoked dress. These had been recommended from the 1870s as a way of avoiding the discomforts of tight waists – the heroine of L. M. Alcott's *Eight Cousins*, 1875, is given the choice between a fashionable dress with a corset and a smock dress with knickerbockers, and chooses the latter – but were not generally popular. By the mid-1890s, however, adult fashions were favouring yoked effects with the interest centred around the shoulders and swelling sleeves. In adult ensembles the fullness falling from the yoke was tightly confined at the waist, but girls' dresses were allowed to hang freely from shoulder to hem (Fig. 86). In spite of the smock shape, smocking as a decorative treatment was not much used. Smock dresses came in all materials and qualities, from the 'knockabout' serge frocks offered in 1895 by John Noble at 1s. 6d. to elaborate hand-embroidered confections. Trimming could be concentrated on the yoke, which might be made up of embroidered tucks or edged with lace flounces. Or it might be spread over the expanses of skirt, as in the example in Fig. 88. The large sleeves of the mid-1890s were always left plain except for an epaulette on the shoulder. For winter, velveteen and plush were favourite fabrics, especially for 'walking dresses' which might double as coats like the earlier pelisses.

Whether a girl wore a smock or one of the more fitted styles thought suitable for older girls, she did not escape the burden of underwear. The miseries caused by corsets to the growing girl have

Fig. 87 Three versions of girls' sailor suits offered by Barran's of Leeds, c. 1900. The second and third have exact copies of boys' sailor jackets.

been graphically described by women growing up before 1920:

> I had a bad figure, and to me they were real instruments of
> torture; they prevented me from breathing, and they dug deep
> holes into my softer parts on every side. (Gwen Raverat,
> b. 1885)[2]

This torture came with the putting on of the first adult-style
boned corset. The experience would be made slightly easier for
girls who had passed in stages from the quilted or corded stays of

*Fig. 88   A small girl's smock dress of
fine cream wool, c. 1895. The front is
hand-embroidered with floral sprays,
and the shoulders are trimmed with
matching bunches of ribbon.*

infancy to corded corsets with steel front and back bones (Fig. 90). As the girl grew, these would be exchanged for longer and shapelier models. Button-on suspenders were allowed as a concession to youth, but were not generally worn by adults until the twentieth century. A range of similar 'soft-corded "Good Sense" corsets' was offered by The Bradford Manufacturing Co. in 1910 in sizes from toddler to adult and priced from 1s. 11d. to 5s. 1d.

Even when made and worn with care, corset-bodices such as these were bound to be both uncomfortable and unhygienic – the metal fastenings would rust if washed. In 1908 an alternative undergarment appeared which introduced a greater degree of freedom and comfort without sacrificing the 'support' which most mothers thought essential (Fig. 91). This was the 'Liberty Bodice', introduced by the corset firm Symingtons of Market Harborough.[3] Like the woollen combinations which had replaced the chemise and drawers, it was made of knitted fabric. Unlike the former, it was made of cotton for ease of washing, and reinforced with strips of woven fabric to help keep its shape. Onto these reinforcing strips were sewn hard rubber buttons to hold petticoats and suspenders. This garment was an immediate success, and was

Fig. 89   Girls' party dresses from Weldon's Bazaar of Children's Fashions, 1912. The different styles are described as suitable for the age ranges 2 to 8, 6 to 12, 10 to 16 and 12 to 18 years.

produced for infants, (wrap-around, no buttons), children and even adults at a rate of up to three million a year. It remained popular throughout the 1920s and 1930s and up to the clothing shortages of the Second World War, when mothers were reduced to making their own from handknitted wool reinforced with tape.[4] After the war the bodice, now without a front opening, fell in popularity until it was discontinued in 1974.

Up to about 1910 girls' clothes continued along the lines set down in the 1890s, with changes mainly affecting details such as the cut of the sleeve and the choice of fabrics and trimming. After 1908, however, there was a drastic change in the silhouette of women's fashion. Skirts which had swept the ground with flaring hems suddenly became narrow, and short enough to show the shoes. The waistline was raised, accentuating the fullness of the bloused bodice. In extreme cases skirts were so tight as to require a slit in the side for walking! This new style was difficult to reconcile with the now accepted ideas of girls' clothing. The narrow skirts would not permit any kind of exercise, while the high-waisted proportions did not look right on dresses which ended at or above the knee.

The result of this change in adult fashion was a split between older and younger girls' styles. These are demonstrated by the engraving shown in Fig. 89, which gives a variety of styles thought suitable for different age groups. There had always been differences between the dresses worn by girls of 3 and 4 and 'young ladies', but previously these had been confined to their length and

Fig. 90 *A small girl's corded corset of cotton sateen, c. 1900. There are buttons at the sides to attach the suspenders. The front and back openings have steel bones. Chest 20 inches (51 cm), waist 18 inches (46 cm), original price 2s. 6d.*

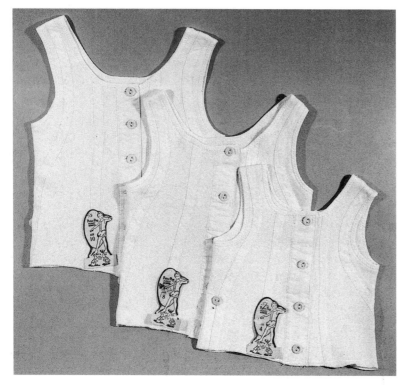

Fig. 91 *Three 'Liberty' bodices from the 1920s with the trade mark 'Peter Pan'. Made from fleecy-backed cotton jersey, reinforced with tape.*

degree of elaboration. Young girls might have more freedom at the waistline, but otherwise were expected to conform to adult styles from the age of 8 upwards. Even the smock dresses of the 1890s needed only a sash at the waist to bring them within the bounds of adult fashion. The old-fashioned smock shape was still used after 1910, though mostly for very small girls up to 4. Girls aged 6 to 10 could have a more modern version of the style, with a square yoke and fullness arranged in box pleats to give a flatter effect. With this was worn a low belt or sash which gave these dresses a long waist and short skirt – the reverse of fashionable proportions! Between the ages of 10 and 16, girls were allowed something nearer to adult styles, with a high-waisted bloused bodice. 'Pinafore' effects were in fashion for adults and children, with a lighter weight fabric used for the neckline and sleeves. These might be detachable for washing, in which case they were called a 'guimpe' or 'chemisette'. The dresses worn at this age differed from those of older girls and women in having calf-length skirts cut with gores to give fullness. From the age of 12 upwards, a girl would progress to young ladies' fashions. These differed from the adult in being slightly simpler, less low-cut for evening wear, and shorter. Even with the hem above the ankle, the narrow straight-cut skirt would make anything faster than a stroll practically impossible.

One of the interesting points about Fig. 89 is the overlap between the age groups mentioned (10 to 16 and 12 to 18 years). This represents an attempt by the pattern and dress manufacturers to rethink their sizings. These had previously been based on age, with a sudden jump to sizing by waist measurement (starting at 22 inches (56 cm)!) once a grown-up figure was attained. The new sizings were meant to cater for girls who were the same age but at different stages of physical maturity. The rate of development was often directly related to social class, and could be cruelly apparent in the comfortably-off households where teenage daughters and young maids-of-all-work lived under the same roof:

> I was small for fifteen and their own daughter, who was thirteen, had reached pubescence and I had not; I was never treated as a child in any way, or even as a young person. (Edith Hall, 1923)[5]

The problem of clothing teenage daughters was solved for many mothers by the gradual acceptance of the 'gymslip' as the most appropriate outfit for schoolgirls. As the name suggests, these had originally been designed for gymnastics, one of the few energetic sports allowed to late nineteenth-century girls.[6] Gradually their use spread through the school day and by the 1920s they had become standard wear in most girls' schools. From the outset they were made of navy wool serge, considered particularly 'healthful' and durable because of its long association with seaside clothing (Fig. 92). They were always sleeveless, with a (generally square) yoke, a square neck, and a wide body placed in box pleats front and back. A sash or belt was worn loosely knotted at the hip. Un-

J.C ENID J.C IRIS J.C CLARICE J.C GYM

Fig. 92 Schoolgirl clothes from Harrods, 1917. Two wool dresses (cost 21s. and 49s. 6d.), and an older girl's skirt and blouse (cost 45s.). The gymslip is worn so short that the matching knickers show; it cost 23s. 6d. (without blouse).

derneath was a blouse, generally white and tailored; the collar might be worn open, or closed with a boyish tie. Most revolutionary of all, the gymslip was worn over matching 'regulation' knickers, with elasticated knees which were pulled well down to hide the gap between the stocking top and the regular underwear. Sometimes the skirt was worn short enough to allow the knickers to show, but this depended on current fashion in skirt-lengths and on the age of the wearer.

The gymslip was welcomed by teachers, who liked the uniformity it provided, and by dress reformers, who appreciated its simple, unconstricting lines. But it must have been a mixed blessing both for the girls who had to wear it and for the parents who had to find money for this new item. The contrast in warmth between wool-clad body and shirt-sleeved arms cannot have been comfortable in winter, while the weight of the thick pleats must have felt oppressive in summer. By the 1920s uniforms were compulsory in most private, convent and high schools but not at the old-style elementary schools (Fig. 93).

For working-class parents whose daughter· had been offered a 'free place' at one of these schools, the most important question was whether the family could afford to forego the wages of a child who stayed on at school beyond the minimum leaving age. The costs of uniform and 'extras' were the second most important consideration. These were fairly substantial; in 1917 Harrods charged

£1. 3s. 6d. for the smallest tunic and knickers, and Pryce Jones of Newtown charged £1. 5s. for gymslip and blouse and 12s. 6d. for matching knickers a few years later. Sometimes the cost of attendance meant that the child's only chance of further education had to be sacrificed; or the minimum outfit might be scraped together, but with no money left over for 'extras'. 'There'd been a deluge of rain. I was soaked to the skin and she [teacher] gave me a roasting. Why had I not got on my mac? Well the answer was very simple, because I didn't own one. But one couldn't tell Miss Stoneman that.' (Maude Mundy, 'free-place' scholar, 1927–31.)[7] Some mothers evaded regulations by making the uniform themselves, though this was not approved by the authorities.

By the middle of the 1920s, women's clothing had undergone a complete transformation from its pre-war state. During the war ankle-length 'hobble' dresses had been abandoned in favour of flared, calf-length skirts and jackets. After 1918 the sacklike silhouette became even looser, the waist dropped to hip level, and skirts rose to meet it. By 1925 they had reached the knee! The short skirts and shapeless cut of the new fashions blurred the previous distinctions between women's and children's clothes. These did not disappear completely; girls' dresses were still worn shorter than their mothers', and were usually of simpler materials. Summer dresses in plain cotton or linen might be enlivened with simple embroidery or applique motifs. Here the ideal to follow was not fine stitching and delicate designs, as it had been in 1900. Bold patterns made up of groups of simple stitches were recognized as being much more 'modern' and better suited to the simple, drop-waisted styles (fig. 94).

There was a boom in home dressmaking for adults and children throughout the 1920s and 1930s. This was partly prompted by the simpler cut of the new fashions, which made exact tailoring less necessary. Other factors included the gradual fall in price of sewing machines and the introduction of hire-purchase arrangements which put them within the reach of working families. Some cautious young women even chose a sewing machine in preference to an engagement ring![8] The post-war trend towards smaller families and smaller homes meant that fewer servants were employed and the mistress of the house would have to undertake any mending or making-over herself. The Wall Street Crash of 1929 made even comfortably-off families more cautious with their finances. Less fortunate families were pushed to the edge of survival by the unemployment and short-time working caused by the 'slump' of the 1930s. For these families, children's clothes were still bought second-hand, or 'on the club'.[9]

By 1935 women's clothes had moved away from the simple drop-waisted styles of the 1920s. Skirts were now calf-length and flared, while bodices were fitted to the hip. The most fashionable styles involved complicated bias-cut panels to give a slim and graceful line. As in 1910, the long and fitted line proved unsuitable for young girls whose dresses were still worn above the knee. Once

Fig. 93 A gymslip and blouse worn in 1935 at a convent school in London. The belt could be in a contrasting colour to indicate which school 'house' a girl belonged to.

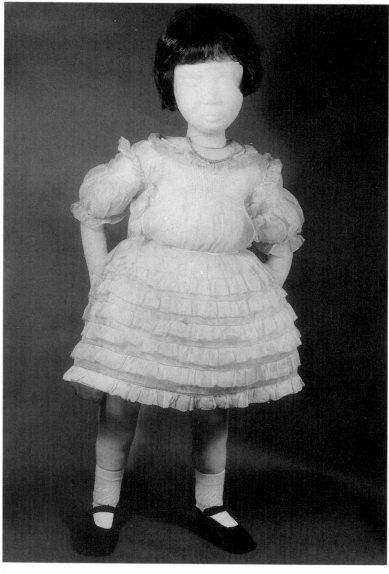

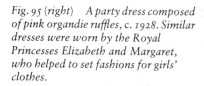

Fig. 94 (*above*) *A linen dress with blue counted-thread embroidery, worn by a girl of nine in 1926. This sleeveless, drop-waisted shape was worn by adults and children in the mid-1920s.*

Fig. 95 (*right*) *A party dress composed of pink organdie ruffles, c. 1928. Similar dresses were worn by the Royal Princesses Elizabeth and Margaret, who helped to set fashions for girls' clothes.*

again the solution was a hierarchy of dress styles, with very short, full smocks for the youngest girls, more fitted, knee-length outfits for the middle age range, and a simplified version of adult fashions for teenagers.

There were two new fashion influences on young girls' clothes in the 1930s. One was the American child star Shirley Temple, who made her debut in 1934 at the age of 6.[10] Her appeal was based on her extreme youth, emphasised by her short 'little girl' dresses and golden ringlets. The influence of these dresses was felt through the cinema screen, through 'Shirley Temple' dolls, and through American dressmaking patterns.[11] The other major influence on girls' clothes was the appearance of two Royal Princesses, Elizabeth and Margaret, born in 1926 and 1930. They received a surprising amount of press publicity, even though they were not in the direct line of succession until the abdication of their uncle Edward VIII in 1936. They were frequently photographed wearing party dresses made up of multiple frills of pink organdy or ribbon. Although these dresses looked luxuriously fragile, they could in fact be made at home by any mother with money to buy the raw materials and patience to hem all the tiny frills! (Fig. 95)[12]

The Second World War and after

By 1939, the taste for feminine frills was beginning to decline, replaced by more tailored styles with wide padded shoulders. There was also an interest in European folk art, expressed through gathered 'peasant' blouses and embroidered 'Tyrolean' cardigans. The coming of war and the restrictions of rationing and Utility reinforced both of these trends. Short, full-skirted smocks were still permitted for babies and toddlers, though they might be made from mother's unwanted petticoat or overall. For older girls, the most economical styles were tailored, with flared panels replacing pleats in the skirt. Skirts and blouses or jumpers were an obvious way of stretching fabric and coupons, as were real or false pinafore and waistcoat effects. Knitting wool was also rationed (two ounces per coupon), so fine knitting was more necessary than ever.

Fig. 96   A girl's siren suit of thick navy-blue wool with a front zip, 1940–45. These were designed to be pulled on quickly during night-time air-raids. A suit like this might cost 16s. to 18s.

Fig. 97   A girl's dress of plain and
checked blue rayon, c. 1950–55.
'Waistcoat' and two-tone effects were
popular during and after the war as
ways round fabric shortages. A similar
dress sold for 25s. in 1953.

Mothers who were better at knitting than sewing were encouraged to make a knitted bodice to extend a too-small dress. Sometimes the results of this 'make-do and mend' overcame the limitations of time, money and coupons (Colour Plate 7), but more often they must have looked and felt very makeshift. Many schools continued to insist on uniform in spite of the hardships caused by bombings and evacuation. Some had already switched to a more modern, un-pleated pinafore, but in most the pleated gymslip was still required.

By the end of the war, women were crying out for a change from strictly tailored suits and wartime austerity. Dior's 'New Look' of 1947 seemed to express everyone's ideal of the post-war woman: feminine, full-skirted, small-waisted and totally unsuited for heavy work at home or in the factory. Girls' dresses followed this new silhouette with fuller skirts and more emphasis on the waistline, though fabric rationing continued until 1949 and the Utility re-strictions until 1952. Some of the dodges learnt during the war such as contrasting 'waistcoat' fronts and false 'pinafore' bodices were still in use in the early 1950s (Fig. 97).

The early 1950s were a period of contradictory influences, several of which can be seen in girls' clothes. Two Royal events – the marriage of Princess Elizabeth in 1947 and her coronation as Queen in 1953 – released a tide of patriotism. This was expressed by the choice of national emblems to decorate printed rayon dresses and homemade knitwear (Fig. 98).[13] There was also a return to the traditional dresses with puffed sleeves and bands of smocking that had been popular in the 1930s (Colour Plate 7).

At the same time, there was a great demand for modernity and novelty in dress. This was satisfied by the use of new materials such as flocked nylon. It also led to the influx of American-designed fashions. The American clothing industry had several ad-vantages over the British; it had not suffered so much in the war, it had less to fear from foreign competition, and the greater potential market led to more accurate sizing and economies of scale. While imported clothing was beyond the reach of most British parents, it helped to set the standard for home-produced goods.

America has been credited with the invention of the teenager, though the word was being used in Britain by the 1940s. It would be truer to say that American teenage styles of the 1950s created a model to which British girls aspired. The extremes of 'bobbysoxer' fashions, with oversized boys' team jackets and full skirts held out by a mass of petticoats, were ignored by most girls. But by the early 1960s goods as diverse as nylons and knitting wool were being directed at the teenage market, with advertising showing teenage entertainments such as record parties.[14]

The 'youth explosion' of the mid-1960s threw up a new group of role-models for young people. Although there had been teenage singers and fashion models before, they had always tried to look older than their years. Twiggy, the model Lesley Hornby, was 17 when she was named 'The face of '66' and 'Woman of the Year'.[15]

Fig. 98 (left)   A rayon sun-dress printed with Coronation motifs, 1953. The border shows a Royal procession, and the scattered motifs include crowns and drums. The matching bolero is a feature often found in women's outfits.

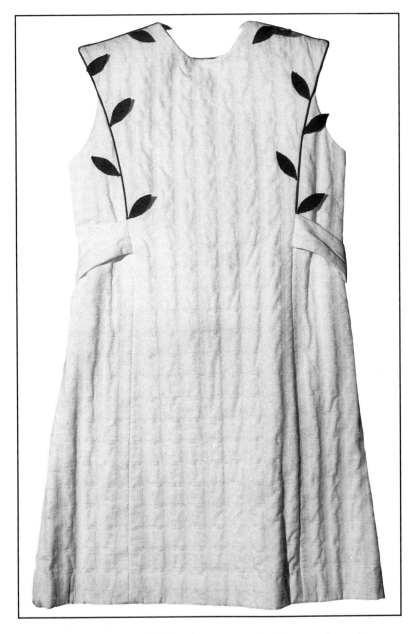

Fig. 99 (right)   A waffle cotton dress with applied 'leaf' trimming, c. 1968. The A-line shape and crisp decoration are typical of mid-1960s fashions. Made by Florence Eisemann, New York.

Her undeveloped, stick-like figure was ideally suited to the new, short-skirted fashions turned out by designers like Mary Quant.

The new dresses for girls and women were short, as little girls' dresses had been for decades, but less fitted. Two favourite styles were the Empire-line, with a flared skirt and high, yoked bodice, and the 1920s revival, with a dropped waist and short pleated skirt. There were also innovations such as the disposable dress made from non-woven material (Fig. 100) – this was supposed to be ideal for holidays – and the see-through crochet dress worn over a matching petticoat. However, these co-existed with more traditional cotton dresses with full skirts and fitted bodices (Fig. 116).

Fig. 100   A disposable 'paper' dress, printed with bright pink daisies, 1967. Marketed under the name 'The Dispo Kid', these dresses were popular with mothers but were withdrawn because of concern for their flammability.

Trousers, in the form of slacks or stretchy ski pants were now fashionable for women's and girls' casual wear (Fig. 101), but they were still rigidly forbidden for school and formal occasions such as church.

By the mid-1970s fashions had turned from the youthful and determinedly modern styles of the previous decade to a look based on fantasy and nostalgia. Denim was taken back to its Western roots with 'cowgirl' skirts and waistcoats worn with checked shirts. A simple skirt and blouse might be given a new twist by making the skirt tiered and pairing it with a 'peasant' shawl or bolero. A taste for nostalgia was satisfied by flowery party dresses, often made long and with Victorian touches, and by the revival of the sailor suit. Several clothing firms built up international reputations by catering for this demand.

The other major influence in the 1970s was sportswear, and garments previously confined to athletic meetings began to appear in high streets and even in discos. Tracksuits, sweatshirts, and stretchy leggings are now so commonly worn by babies and adults that it is difficult to see what distinguishes the girl's version from her mother's. Girls' clothes tend to have well-defined surface patterns – spots, stripes or flowers – self-consciously feminine details such as bows and frills, and often incorporate the images of favourite cartoon characters.

Fig. 101   A nylon anorak printed with psychedelic patterns in shades of blue and purple, worn with pale-blue acrylic jersey 'hipster' trousers, c. 1970. These were smart casual clothes for a girl of 11. Similar anoraks cost £4 in 1966.

What is more significant than the clothes themselves is the way in which they are being marketed: magazines aimed at pre-pubescent girls now include pages of fashion and beauty advice. Even younger girls can have toy beauty salons and pretend make-up. It seems as if, notwithstanding their improved chances of education and rewarding employment, most girls are happy to envisage a future spent as wives and mothers.

The RANGER PLAYSUITS

Make the Children Happy

Boys: 1890-1985

Many of the typically Edwardian features of boys' clothing were already established by 1890, including such distinctive outfits as the sailor suit. There was still a strict hierarchy leading from the toddler's dress through suits with knickerbockers or short trousers to the full suit, which boys first wore in their mid-teens. But this transition was becoming blurred through the adoption of more tailored styles for even the youngest boys. This was partly through the influence of adult fashion, with 'tailor-mades' all the rage for smart young women. But it is also a testimony to the efficiency of the ready-to-wear firms who were able to provide small tailored garments more cheaply than a personal tailor, and more efficiently than a dressmaker.

Most of these outfits were based either on the sailor suit or on the 'Norfolk' suit, with stitched down pleats and a cloth belt. Styles and materials were interchanged to give hybrids such as the tweed sailor suit or the Norfolk suit with a sailor collar (Fig. 106). Older boys might have a suit with an open jacket and waistcoat. Both these and the Norfolk suits would be worn with a starched turn-down collar: sailor suits were worn with a collarless vest.

Very young boys' outfits had a skirt pleated like a kilt, combined with a sailor blouse (Fig. 105). As well as making tailored suits, some of the mass manufacturers had expanded into knitted jerseys and shorts.[1] These had advantages for both manufacturer and consumer: they were cheaper to manufacture, with fewer parts to cut, and less skilled labour needed; they would stretch to fit a growing child; and they could be washed. By the mid-1880s, Leicester-based firms were turning out sports jerseys, caps and jackets in children's and adult sizes.[2] Knitted jerseys might be used for everyday to save wear and tear on 'best suits'. In wealthier families they would be worn for active sports only, with Norfolk suits for country and informal wear, a 'Rugby' suit with plain jacket and knickerbockers for school and an 'Eton' suit for 'best'.

The use of famous schools' names for the different styles reflects the extent to which the smaller private schools attempted to follow their famous models in imposing uniformity of behaviour and of dress. The Eton suit was actually based on the uniform worn at that establishment, with a short pointed jacket which derived from prototypes of the 1820s (Fig. 64). The Eton suit was imposed on many small boys for best wear up to the 1920s, but did not always create the desired effect (Fig. 109).

By 1910 the complete sailor suit was gradually fading in popularity, though sailor trimmings were still used for small boys. Young boys' outfits had moved on from the blouse and kilt to a low-waisted tunic worn over shorts. These were usually made in 'masculine' fabrics such as serge, linen or piqué to distinguish them from babies' dresses.

There was also a recognition that small boys might need play-clothes, and for this sets of knitted jerseys and shorts were invaluable. Some were advertised in Harrods' catalogue for 1919 in

Fig. 102 (above)   Three pairs of 'everyday' shoes. A pair of clogs with irons, late nineteenth to early twentieth-century; a pair of button boots, worn by young boys and girls c. 1880–1900; and a pair of Utility lace-up shoes.

Fig. 103   Part of a boy's suit of coarse cream wool with a blue check, c. 1890–1920. It is strongly but cheaply made, with no lining. It may have been worn by a boy just starting work.

The Norfolk, Fig. 55. The Brighton, Fig. 57. The New York, Fig. 56. The Sydenham, Fig. 58.

Fig. 104 Popular styles for boys from The Cutter's Practical Guide, c. 1900. The pleats on Norfolk jackets were added to allow for movement when shooting or fishing. Boys' styles such as the 'Brighton' often had strips of fabric stitched on instead of pleats. Note the high-heeled button boots shown on two of the figures.

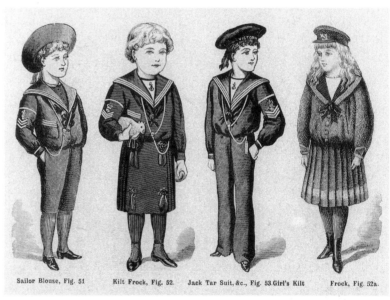

Sailor Blouse, Fig. 51. Kilt Frock, Fig. 52. Jack Tar Suit, &c., Fig. 53.Girl's Kilt Frock, Fig. 52a.

Fig. 105 Four variants of the sailor suit from the same book. The second combines a sailor blouse with a kilted skirt for a small boy. The third is a 'Jack Tar' or 'Man o' War' suit. The fourth is a girl's version (see Chapter 8).

attractive shades of rayon and wool including pink, champagne, rose, grey and amethyst at a cost of 13s. 6d. Made with a turndown collar and buttoned neck, these jerseys could be passed on to sisters to wear with a skirt, and survived in identical form until the 1950s (Fig. 110).

An even more practical garment for play was the 'Romper Combination Overall' (Fig. 108), offered by Harrods in 1917 from 3s. 11d. to 7s. 11d. This was a larger version of the baby's 'crawling overall' introduced at the same time (see Chapter 7), but did not share its success.

A popular outfit which first made its appearance during the First World War was the 'buster' suit.[3] This came in two variants, both consisting of a pair of shorts and a contrasting blouse. In one

Fig. 106 A class of boys at a board school in Putney, 1896. The majority wear either Norfolk or sailor suits – one of these is in tweed, with a velvet collar! Other choices are a bloused jacket with a wide turn-down collar, and an adult-style three-piece suit. One boy wears a striped jersey.

version, the buster suit proper, the shorts were held up by braces of the same fabric. In the other, the shorts buttoned onto the waist of the blouse.

These were both considered suitable as a first shorts suit for a boy as young as 2, perhaps as a 'best' alternative to the tunic and shorts. In both instances the shorts differed from older boys' trousers in being held up by buttoning to a bodice, not by braces, and in having a flap back rather than a front fly. The shorts-and-blouse suit may have derived some of its inspiration from the skeleton suit; two of the examples in Harrods' catalogue are called 'Greenaway' after the artist Kate Greenaway who was famous for her illustrations of Regency boys and girls.

These suits remained popular throughout the 1930s and 1940s, and were executed in a great variety of materials. They were made of machine-knitted wool, or knitted at home from artificial silk (Fig. 111). Fancier examples had velvet shorts and a silk or satin blouse decorated with smocking or a frilled collar. Plain versions made from linen-look rayon were advertised by Grattan in 1954 for 14s.

In the late 1920s and early 1930s a greater degree of informality reached menswear. This was encouraged by the example of Edward, Prince of Wales (Edward VIII). His taste for elaborate Fair Isle golfing jumpers set a fashion for men and boys which could easily be copied (Fig. 112). Other garments which crossed over from sportswear at this time were pleated flannel trousers with turn-ups and wool blazers (originally worn for cricket). By the end of the 1920s, flannel trousers or shorts and blazers had

Fig. 107 (*right*)   *A young boy's tunic and shorts made by Barran's of Leeds, c. 1910. Known as the 'Clyde' suit, this style sold for about 18s. in sizes to fit 3- to 6-year-olds.*

Fig. 108. (*below*)   *A 'Romper Combination Overall' in blue linen, sold by Harrods at 3s. 11d. to 7s. 11d. in 1917. This example is one of a set of five worn by two brothers aged 5 and 6.*

Fig. 109 *The Eton suit as worn by the immortal William Brown in a drawing by Thomas Henry, 1920. The starched collar has come adrift, and the trousers are creased and stained. The boy on the right is the same age as William but is still in an embroidered tunic.*

Fig. 110 *A boy of 5 wearing a classic button-front jersey and shorts, 1925. Jerseys like this remained extremely popular for school and play wear until the 1950s. Lace-up shoes have now taken the place of boots.*

become official or unofficial uniform for most schoolboys. The Army and Navy Stores were charging between £1 and £2. 10s. for a suit like this in 1929. Both shorts and trousers were now held up with a belt rather than braces, making life much more comfortable! Boys' formal suits were often made of material and with detailing similar to their fathers', even when these were inappropriate. When the square shoulders and wide lapels of 1930s and 1940s men's jackets were combined with short trousers, the effect was oddly truncated (Fig. 114).

With shorts being worn by toddlers, the great distinction in boys' clothing was no longer between dresses or tunics and trousers, but between short and long trousers. 'Longs' were usually put on in the mid-teens, an age which coincided with that of entry into the working world. Some secondary and grammar schools imposed a height qualification for wearing long trousers, and others insisted that even the eldest boys should wear shorts.

Fig. 111 (right) A small boy's buster suit, hand-knitted in yellow rayon, with green smocking across the chest. Made in 1932 for a 2-year-old.

Fig. 112 (below) An elaborately patterned Fair Isle jersey in shades of red, green and fawn, knitted for a schoolboy in 1935.

During the Second World War, boys' clothes were even more difficult to provide than their sisters'. The Utility regulations restricted both the cut and the size of boys' clothing; from 1942 manufacturers were prohibited from making long trousers in sizes smaller than 11 years.[4] Shirts and jumpers could be made at home, saving four coupons apiece. Young boys' buster suits could be cut down from adult cast-offs. Wartime mothers were urged to make 'smart knickers for the little boy from his old summer coat', to be paired with a blouse cut down from 'one of daddy's old shirts' (Fig. 113).[5] These suits were especially popular during the war because of the scarcity of elastic for waistbands. Once the war ended, shorts suits with elasticated waists gradually superseded the older types with buttons or braces.

By the early 1950s, boys' clothing had been much simplified from the early years of the century. The standard progression was now from rompers to shorts suits (worn from the age of 2 or younger) and then to the standard jersey and shorts or shirt and shorts of the schoolboy. There was a range of casual clothes avail-

Fig. 113   A small boy's braces suit with pink linen shorts and a red gingham shirt, c. 1940. These suits were often made at home, though this example was mass-produced.

SUITS FOR BOYS

Our Agents must allow Customers a Discount of 9d. in the £ on all Cash purchases

Fig. 114   Boys' double-breasted suits from Grattan's catalogue for 1949. The adult details of squared shoulders and wide lapels contrast strangely with the shorts.

able to boys, including lumber jackets (an adaptation of wartime uniform), cotton jersey sports shirts and T-shirts, and dungarees. Even some outfits which looked formal were adapted for the comfort of their young wearers, by the addition of shoulder straps to trousers, for example.

During the 1950s a strong element of fantasy became apparent in small boys' clothes. Some of the themes were based on American popular culture: parents could indulge their offspring with 'playsuits' in the characters of Cowboys, Indians, and Davy Crockett. Another strand was an interest in 'space age' technology reflected in knitting patterns for 'jet plane' helmets and gloves, with earflaps and palms shaped like fins.[6] A more subdued vein of invention was seen in shirts intended for holiday wear, which were printed with seaside, cowboy, Hawaiian or Mexican motifs (Fig. 115).

American influence has also been claimed for the 1950s phenomenon of the teenager. It was a concept firmly based in the

Fig. 115 A holiday set of elasticated shorts and shirt, printed with a pattern of fishermen on a bright red background. Worn by a 4-year-old in 1966.

economy of the decade, with young school-leavers able to earn relatively high wages. A portion of this was free for spending on pop records and clothes to suit the cult of the moment. The first 'youth culture' music was American rock and roll, whose followers wore jeans or exaggerated 'Teddy Boy' suits. Later came British-based Mod music and, of course, the Beatles.

Younger boys were not able to indulge so heavily in records or extreme clothing, but some 'modern' styles did filter down. Among these were Mod jerkins in imitation leather, and V-necked pullovers worn with polo-necked shirts. Boys' suits became slimmer-fitting, and might be made of shiny mixed fabrics instead of tweed or flannel.

The American youth culture movements of the late 1960s were very different from those of 15 years earlier. Enthusiasts of 'flower power' urged people to defy convention in their behaviour and their clothes, relax and 'find themselves'. These ideas had a noticeable effect on fashionable menswear, which became more colourful, less tailored, and more varied in its materials. Trousers were worn at hip-level and closely fitted except for the flared hems. Loosely-cut shirts could be worn with flowered cravats or startling kipper ties. Favourite colours were burgundy, pink and orange, all

Fig. 116   A group of 6-year-olds in 1967. Most of the boys are wearing either open-necked sports shirts or the more modern T-shirts. The girls' dresses are divided between the full-skirted styles of the 1950s and the more modern drop-waisted or flared shapes. Both boys and girls wear T-bar sandals.

of which had previously been considered unsuitable for grown men. In a reversal of the nineteenth-century practice, these adult styles were considered too extreme for boys. Their influence was felt only faintly, in the use of a textured fabric for a suit, in the loud stripes of a shirt or the floral patterns of a tie (Fig. 117).

The styles which followed these aesthetic and sometimes effeminate fashions were more sharply-defined and more based on a traditional idea of masculinity. This was expressed through squarer tailoring and stiffer fabrics. By far the most important of these was denim, which was now manufactured in a huge variety of styles and garments. Another favourite was wide-ribbed corduroy. These fabrics had both been traditionally associated with working clothes, but were cut off from their past by the use of exaggerated cut and bright colours (Fig. 118).

Both adults and children were learning to look at the label on a garment, not its material, and cults developed around different brands of jeans. These enthusiasms were lost on the education authorities, who maintained a strict 'no denim' rule in most schools. A phenomenon of the 1970s was the entry of adult fashion designers into the children's market. One of the first to do this was Mary Quant, who had previously dressed adults to resemble elon-

Fig. 117   A boy's suit of the 1960s,
showing some of the new freedom
affecting menswear. The suit is of
chunky fawn wool, and is worn with a
yellow and green striped shirt and a
yellow floral tie.

Fig. 118   A boy's suit designed by
Mary Quant in 1977 using 'fun' fabrics
– gold corduroy, yellow canvas and
mustard viyella. Long 'shorts' with
turnups were briefly fashionable for
women as well as boys. The shirt
sleeves have no cuffs, and were
probably intended to be worn rolled
up. Length 28.5 inches (72 cm).

gated children (Fig. 118). She was soon folowed by more traditional firms such as Christian Dior.[7]

Now it seems as if children are even more fashion-conscious
than their parents. A great range of clothing styles and prices is
available, from mock-Victorian sailor suits to casual sweatsuits.
The latter are usually embellished with the names or pictures of
currently fashionable television heroes or toys, from Postman Pat
to Rambo. Older boys can insist on clothes from one of the many
high street chains which offer scaled-down fashion for chidren.

After centuries during which parents chose their children's
clothes, ignoring all opposition, the shoe is now on the other foot.
The child population is now proportionally low, owing to a de-
clining birthrate, but the period legally defined as childhood is
longer than ever before. Products aimed at children seem to
occupy an increasingly large place in national and family economies, even when the latter are severely strained. Perhaps there is a
value in scarcity, or perhaps these children are just being educated
into their primary duty as citizens of the twenty-first century – that
of consumption.

Notes

Chapter 1

1 William Cadogan, *An Essay Upon Nursing, and the Management of Children*, London, 1748, p. 10.
2 J. J. Rousseau, *Emile*, Everyman Editions, 1975, p. 10.
3 Michael Underwood, *On the Diseases of Children*, London, 1784, p. 230.
4 Ibid., p. 180.
5 Ibid., p. 228.
6 See E. Lipton, A. Steinschneider and J. Richmond, 'Swaddling, a Child Care Practice', *Pediatrics*, vol. 35, No. 3, March 1965.
7 P. Cunnington and A. Buck, *Children's Costume in England 1300–1900*, A & C Black, 1965, pp. 68–9.
8 The tax continued until 1853. See Caroline Davidson, *A Woman's Work is Never Done*, Chatto and Windus, 1982, p. 125.
9 There is a set like this in the collections of York Castle Museum.
10 See E. D. H. Johnson, *Paintings of the British Social Scene*, Weidenfeld and Nicholson, 1986, pp. 80 *et seq.* for a discussion of 'sensibility'.
11 A. Buck, *Dress in 18th Century England*, Batsford, 1979, pp. 110–11.
12 In the collections of Bath Museum of Costume, and The Whitworth Art Gallery, Manchester.
13 Buck, op. cit., pp. 192–3.
14 Ibid., pp. 194–5.
15 The bodice of a baby-sized 'bib-fronted' dress survives in the collections of Stoke-on-Trent Museum.
16 See Zoffany's portrait of Lord Willoughby de Broke and family, *c.* 1767, in E. Ewing, *History of Children's Costume*, Batsford, 1977, fig. 29.
17 M. Swain, *The Flowerers*, Chambers, 1955, pp. 22–6.

Chapter 2

1 See *Children in an Interior* by Devis, cat. No. 8, in E. D'Oench, *Arthur Devis*, Yale Center for British Art, 1980.
2 See a letter of 1759, cited in Cunnington and Buck, op. cit., p. 127.
3 Buck, op. cit., p. 22.
4 Cited in Cunnington and Buck, op. cit., p. 129.
5 See the portraits of the Gwillym and Vanneck families, cat. Nos. 15 and 29, D'Oench, op. cit.
6 See *Mrs Barclay with her Children* and *The Wilkinson Family*, cat. Nos. 16 and 20, M. Webster, *Francis Wheatley*, The Paul Mellon Foundation for British Art, 1970.
7 Webster, op. cit., cat. Nos. 4, 22, 27.
8 Webster, op. cit., cat. Nos. 5, 16, 27, 30, 33, 43.

9 Buck, op. cit., p. 198.
10 Johnson, op. cit., p. 112.
11 A. Ribeiro, *Dress and Morality*, Batsford, 1986, pp. 115–6.
12 In the collection of the Gallery of English Costume, Manchester. Illustrated in Buck, op. cit., Fig. 18.
13 Formerly on loan to the Whitney Museum of American Art, New York.
14 There is an example of this type in the collections of York Castle Museum.
15 See Susan Sibbald's 'Memoirs', cited in N. Waugh, *Corsets and Crinolines*, Batsford, 1987, p. 130.
16 See the conversation between Princess Charlotte of Wales, and one of her ladies in 1811, cited in Cunnington and Buck, op. cit., p. 197.
17 Buck, op. cit., p. 198.

Chapter 3

1 See Hogarth's engravings *Noon* and *Evening*, 1736, Johnson, op. cit., Figs. 3 and 4.
2 Buck, op. cit., p. 50.
3 Used as the epigraph to Locke's *Some Thoughts Concerning Education*, 1693.
4 Rousseau, op. cit., p. 91.
5 In the Kunsthistorisches Museum, Vienna.
6 Rousseau, op. cit., p. 91.
7 *c.* 1756. Formerly on loan to the National Portrait Gallery, London.
8 In the Louvre.
9 See Wheatley's *Ralph Winstanley Wood and Son*, 1787, cat. No. 59, Webster, op. cit.
10 From the *Journal des Luxus und der Moden*, 1787, in the print collection of the Victoria and Albert Museum.
11 Fig. 58 in Johnson, op. cit.
12 An earlier example is Hoppner's 1798 portrait of *Lady Ann Lambton and Her Children*, in the collection of the Earl of Durham.
13 *Four Hundred Years of Fashion*, The Victoria and Albert Museum, Collins, 1984, cat. No. 33.
14 *The Workwoman's Guide*, by A Lady, 1840, reprinted by Bloomfield Books, 1975, Plate 7.
15 For example, a drawing by R. R. Reinagle dated 1815.
16 Charles Dickens, *Sketches by Boz*, 1836; 'Meditations in Monmouth Street'.

Chapter 4

1 See the 1921 layette reproduced in S. Blum, *Everyday Fashions of the '20s*, Dover, 1981, p. 45.
2 *The Workwoman's Guide*, reprinted by Bloomfield

Books, 1975, p. 33.

3 See M. Swain, *The Flowerers*, Chambers, 1955, for a full account of this industry. A brief summary can be found in the same author's *Ayrshire and Other Whitework*, Shire Publications, 1982.

4 M. Swain, *Ayrshire and Other Whitework*, Shire Publications, 1982.

5 See S. Levey, *Lace, a History*, Victoria and Albert Museum, 1983. p. 80.

6 *The Workwoman's Guide*, reprinted by Bloomfield Books, 1975, p. 26.

7 Cadogan, op. cit., p. 11.

8 *The Workwoman's Guide*, reprinted by Bloomfield Books, 1975, Plate 4.

9 Ibid., pp. 38–9.

10 H. Mayhew, *The Morning Chronicle Survey of Labour and the Poor*, reprinted by Caliban Books 1982, vol. 6, p. 133.

11 M. Swain, *Ayrshire and Other Whitework*, Shire Publications, 1982, p. 24.

12 M. Swain, *The Flowerers*, Chambers, 1955, p. 52.

13 M. Swain, *Ayrshire and Other Whitework*, Shire Publications, 1982, p. 25.

14 *Four Hundred Years of Fashion*, The Victoria and Albert Museum, Collins, 1984, pp. 38–9.

15 Cunnington and Buck, op. cit., p. 124.

16 *Cassell's Household Guide*, vol. I, p. 370.

17 Ibid., vol. I, p. 291.

18 Ibid., vol. I, p. 293.

19 *Mrs Leach's Children's and Young Ladies' Dressmaker*, June, 1886.

20 P. Robertson (ed.), *The Shell Book of Firsts*, Ebury Press, 1983.

Chapter 5

1 *Four Hundred Years of Fashion*, The Victoria and Albert Museum, Collins, 1984, cat. No 35.

2 *Casselll's Household Guide*, vol. II, pp. 75–6.

3 See F. Thompson, *Lark Rise to Candleford*, Oxford University Press, 1984, p. 158.

4 *Cassell's Household Guide*, vol. II, p. 196.

5 Cited by an outworker receiving 2s. for a day's work. Mayhew, op. cit., vol. 6, p. 136.

6 *The Workwoman's Guide*, reprinted by Bloomfield Books, 1975, Introduction.

7 Catalogue of Pryce Jones of Newtown, Wales, c. 1918–20.

8 M. Hughes, *A London Family, 1870–1900*, Oxford University Press, 1946, p. 184.

9 Ewing, op. cit., pp. 119–122.

10 S. Levitt, *The Victorians Unbuttoned*, George Allen and Unwin, 1986, pp. 121–4.

11 C. Walkley, *The Way to Wear 'em*, Peter Owen, 1985, fig. 35.

12 Levitt, op. cit., pp. 125–6.

Chapter 6

1 *Cassell's Household Guide*, vol. II, p. 361.

2 P. Byrde, *The Male Image*, Batsford, 1979, p. 85.

3 *Four Hundred Years of Fashion*, The Victoria and Albert Museum, Collins, 1984, p. 31.

4 E. Ewing, *History of Children's Costume*, Batsford, 1977, Fig. 47.

5 Johnson, op. cit., Fig. 37.

6 *The Workwoman's Guide*, reprinted by Bloomfield Books, 1975, Plate 19 and p. 119.

7 There is an example in green tartan velvet in the collections of Carlisle Museum.

8 Ewing, op. cit., Fig. 54.

9 Women also wore zouave jackets – see the Oxford English Dictionary: zouave. 2.

10 There is a fashionplate of 1868 showing this ensemble in the collection of The Fashion Research Centre, Bath.

11 See J. Burnett (ed.), *Destiny Obscure*, Allen Lane, 1982, pp. 135–70 for a full account of nineteenth-century educational provision.

12 See Thomas Brooks' *The Captured Truant*, 1850, Fig. 135 in Johnson, op. cit.

13 Information supplied by the Royal Naval Museum, Portsmouth.

14 An advertisement, c. 1878, in the archives of the Museum of London.

15 Cited in Burnett, op. cit., p. 63.

16 Ibid., p. 305.

17 Frank Meadow Sutcliffe, *Morning and Evening*, 1884.

Chapter 7

1 Mrs S. Frankenburg, *Common Sense in the Nursery*, 1922, reprinted 1946, Penguin, p. 111.

2 S. Fox M.D., *Mother and Baby*, J & A Churchill, 1912, p. 32.

3 A. Miall, *Making Clothes for Children*, Pitman, 1934, p. 24.

4 Fashion plate of 1868 in the collections of York Castle Museum.

5 Dr A. Bowley CBE, *Wages and Income in the United Kingdom Since 1860*, Cambridge University Press, 1937, Table XI.

6 Miall, op. cit., p. 15.

7 *Cassell's Household Guide*, vol. I, p. 243.

8 J. Paoletti and S. Thompson, 'Gender Differences in Rompers and Creepers', paper presented to the Costume Society of America, 1987.

9 Available in Britain in revised editions from 1918 to the 1950s.

10 Thompson, op. cit., p. 131.

11 A. Guppy, *Children's Clothes 1939–1970*, Blandford, 1978, p. 97. This book gives a detailed account of the regulations affecting children's clothes during World War II.

12 Miall, op. cit., p. 14.

13 Ewing, op. cit., pp. 172–3.

14 There is an example of a 1920s 'Stork' nappy in the collections of Bethnal Green Museum of Childhood, London.

15 Frankenburg, op. cit., pp. 110–4.

Chapter 8

1 There is a set of matching sailor suits worn by a

brother and sister in the late 1920s in the collection of Bethnal Green Museum of Childhood, London.

2 G. Raverat, *Period Piece*, Faber 1952, p. 259.

3 C. Page, *Foundations of Fashion*, Leicestershire Museums, 1981, pp. 75–8.

4 J. Koster and M. Murray, *Modern Knitting Illustrated*, Odhams, 1945, pp. 167–9.

5 Cited in G. Braybon and P. Summerfield, *Out of The Cage*, Pandora 1987, p. 142.

6 Ewing, op. cit., pp. 117–25.

7 Cited in P. Summerfield, 'An Oral History of Schooling in Lancashire 1900–50', *Oral History*, vol. 15, No. 2, pp. 19–31, 1987.

8 See Burnett, op. cit., p. 253.

9 See ibid., p. 322.

10 Ewing, op. cit., p. 134.

11 The Butterick Fashion Magazine for Summer 1935 featured a paper doll based on Shirley Temple.

12 See Molly Weir's autobiography, *Shoes Were for Sunday*, Pan, 1973, pp. 82–3.

13 Patterns for 'Coronation' knitwear were issued by several companies, including Weldon's and Marriner.

14 There was a popular brand of stockings called 'Teens hit parade' in the mid-1960s. See P. Everett, *You'll Never be 16 Again*, B.B.C. Publications, 1986.

15 J. Harris, S. Hyde and G. Smith, *1966 and All That*, Trefoil, 1986, p. 46.

Chapter 9

1 Information from a book of photographs, showing designs registered by John Barran and Sons of Leeds, now in the collections of the Gallery of English Costume, Manchester.

2 Levitt, op. cit., p. 124.

3 Supposedly called after the cartoon character Buster Brown, who actually wore a tunic. See Ewing, op. cit. pp. 131–2.

4 Guppy, op. cit., p. 117.

5 *Woman and Home* magazine, 1942.

6 From a knitting pattern in the collections of Bristol Museums.

7 See L. M. Taggart, 'Designer Children', *The Sunday Times Magazine*, 28 Feb., 1988.

Glossary

Ayrshire work   A type of very fine white needlework, using mostly textured stitches. Its distinctive feature is cut-out areas filled with needle lace. Made in Scotland 1814–1860s, and imitated elsewhere. Used for baby garments and adult accessories.

barra-coat   (Also *barra*, *barrow-coat*). Another name for the day-flannel, usually one made with a wrap-over bodice.

bearing cloth   A large square of heavy silk fabric, often edged with gold lace or embroidery, which was wrapped round a swaddled baby during the christening ceremony (sixteenth to mid eighteenth century).

bed   A rectangle of linen wrapped round a swaddled baby and pinned in place. It kept the arms fixed by the sides and the legs straight.

binder   A piece of linen or flannel wound round a baby's waist to 'support' the back and stomach. Sometimes shaped and quilted like stays. In use up to the 1950s.

breeching   The point when a small boy graduated from petticoats to his first pair of trousers. Often treated as a ceremony. Practiced until the early twentieth century.

broderie anglaise   A type of bold embroidery consisting of different shaped eyelets arranged to form a pattern. Popular 1850–1900, and used for women's and children's underwear and accessories, and babies' dresses.

buster suit   A small boy's suit consisting of shorts and a blouse, the shorts held up either by matching shoulder straps or by buttoning onto the blouse (From *c*. 1915).

cambric   A tightly woven, lightweight fabric made from linen or cotton. Used for underwear and baby garments in the eighteenth and ninteenth centuries.

chemise   The undergarment worn next to the skin by women and children until the early twentieth century. Made of linen, cotton or flannel, with a low neck, short sleeves and a wide body ending at knee level.

chemise gown   A fashionable dress of the 1780s, made of lightweight fabric gathered on drawstrings. At first thought indecent because of its lack of tailoring and resemblance to an undergarment, it eventually found favour with both adults and children.

diaper   A tightly woven linen fabric with a small diamond or other pattern. Used for babies' nappies until the mid nineteenth century. Also used for bibs because of its absorbency.

flannel   A loosely woven wool cloth with a fuzzy surface. Used for babies' underwear from the eighteenth century onwards. 'Day-flannel' and 'night-flannel' were terms for the long flannel petticoats worn by babies throughout the nineteenth and twentieth centuries.

forehead piece   A triangular piece of fabric, decorated with embroidery or with a lace edging. Tied round the head with tapes, it would just show under the front of a baby's cap (sixteenth to mid eighteenth centuries).

holland   A firm, unbleached cotton or linen fabric with a glazed surface, used for soft furnishings in the nineteenth century. Also used for young children's aprons and pinafores.

hollie point   A form of needlelace used to decorate babies' shirts and caps in the eighteenth century. Worked in a grid, with spaces forming the pattern.

leading strings   Cords or strips of fabric sewn to the shoulders of toddlers' dresses to help them learn to walk. Used on older girls' dresses as a symbol of their need for parental guidance. Replaced by leading reins in the nineteenth century.

long stay   A stayband and bib combined, with a panel to cover the baby's body and a strip to go over the head.

muslin   A very fine, loosely woven cotton fabric. Originally imported from Bengal; made in Britain from the 1780s onwards. Used for accessories, for trimming, and for dresses.

organdie   Fine translucent cotton, usually stiffened.

paletot   Originally a loose fitting cloak for men and women. In the nineteenth century a woman's loose fitting jacket.

pelisse   Originally an early nineteenth-century woman's coat, often made of silk with a wool interlining. Used in the mid nineteenth century for young children's coat-dresses with matching capes. In the late nineteenth and early twentieth centuries, a baby's or toddler's caped coat.

redingote   Woman's long coat with a cut-away front, or a front-piece of contrasting material or colour.

robings   Originally flat pleats of fabric which edged the bodice opening of eighteenth-century women's dresses. From 1820–1920, used for the narrow strips of fabric or lace framing the bodice and skirt panels on babies' gowns.

skeleton suit   A small boy's suit with the trousers buttoned on to the waist of the jacket or waistcoat. Usually high-waisted and tight-fitting (1780–1820).

slip   Used from *c.* 1750 to describe a baby's dress made from a single piece of fabric with tucks for shaping. Also used to describe the simple (but tailored) linen dresses worn by older children in the late eighteenth century. Around 1800, applied to coloured silk underdresses worn with transparent net or muslin gowns – hence the present meaning.

stayband   A strip of fabric placed over the head of a swaddled baby and pinned to its shirt. Intended to keep the head straight and to support the neck.

stays   Corsets worn by babies and chidren from the eighteenth century to the early twentieth century. Made from strong linen or 'jean' cotton, stiffened with whalebone, cords or quilting.

Swiss embroidery   Machine embroidery imitating broderie anglaise and other types of whitework. Developed in Switzerland, it began to take over from hand embroidery in the 1860s.

tippet   A shaped shouldercape, often with pointed fronts. Children's were usually made to match a dress or coat (eighteenth to early nineteenth centuries).

tunic   A garment worn by young boys in the nineteenth and early twentieth centuries. It could be made like a coat or like a dress, but was usually differentiated from girls' and toddlers' dresses by its materials, its loose cut, and by features such as an open front skirt. Worn with matching trousers or with long drawers.

Select Bibliography

A LADY, *The Workwoman's Guide*, 1840, reprinted by Bloomfield Books, 1975.

ALDBURGHAM, A., *Yesterday's Shopping* (reprint of 1907 Army & Navy Stores catalogue), David & Charles, 1969.

ALDBURGHAM, A., *Victorian Shopping* (Harrods' Catalogue, 1895), David & Charles, 1972.

BEEKMAN, D., *The Mechanical Baby*, Dennis Dobson, 1977.

BURNETT, J., ed., *Destiny Obscure*, Allen Lane, 1982.

CUNNINGTON, P., and BUCK, A., *Children's Costume in England 1300–1900*, A & C Black, 1965.

EWING, E., *History of Children's Costume*, Batsford, 1977.

THE GALLERY OF ENGLISH COSTUME, MANCHESTER, *Picture Book Number Seven: Children's Costume*, Manchester City Art Gallery, 1959.

GINSBURG, M., *Victorian Dress in Photographs*, Batsford, 1988.

GUPPY, A., *Children's Clothes 1939–1970*, Blandford, 1978.

JOHNSON, E. D. H., *Paintings of the British Social Scene*, Weidenfeld & Nicholson, 1986.

LANGBRIDGE, R., *Edwardian Shopping*, (Army & Navy Stores catalogues from 1898), David & Charles, 1975.

LANSDELL, A., *Fashion à la Carte 1860–1900*, Shire Publications, 1985.

ROUSSEAU, J. J., *Emile*, Everyman Editions, 1975.

SWAIN, M., *The Flowerers*, Chambers, 1955.

SWAIN, M., *Ayrshire and Other Whitework*, Shire Publications, 1982.

TARRANT, N., *The Rise and Fall of the Sleeve*, Royal Scottish Museum, 1983.

THOMPSON, F., *Lark Rise to Candleford*, Oxford University Press, 1984.

VICTORIA AND ALBERT MUSEUM, *Four Hundred Years of Fashion*, Collins, 1984.

WALVIN, J., *A Child's World*, Penguin, 1982.

Index